We're excited you've chosen to read
Stomp the Elephant in the Office.

For more than 20 years, we've been refining processes that serve thousands of leaders around the globe. In the years since this book was written, much has evolved for leaders like you and the global workforce. Some things to consider while reading the book:

- Your organization may not be toxic (congratulations if that's the case). Our goal with this book is to accelerate through challenges regardless of the current state of your culture.
- The term"Wellness Culture" is referenced often in the book. We've upgraded our programs, including the Pathways to Leadership® Process, to reflect our current belief: ownership of your culture includes you crafting a name for your culture that suits your organization.
- An important focus of our work is the "Best Ever" Principle: The ability to realize and activate potential in every interaction, every day. You won't find this mentioned in this book, yet the tools here support this concept and allow you to build best ever experiences at work and home. Look for "best ever" in an upcoming book.

Congratulations on taking the next step in delivering high performance. We look forward to hearing about your successes and ideas for application moving forward.

{ **THE BIG PROMISE: 2 Years in 3 Days.** In three days, we'll accelerate your team's leadership competencies at a rate that would otherwise take two years to accomplish. It's proven, and that's why our flagship process, Pathways to Leadership® is our most requested. }

ABOUT US
Verus Global® equips you to deliver your targeted leadership competencies and values necessary for best ever performance*. **And, we do it like nobody else.**

Best ever performance means you and your team realize and activate potential: an environment of excellence that promotes and delivers continuous people improvement and results. As you consistently live and lead from your values, improved results and fulfillment become the norm.

 verus | global.

more at verusglobal.com

STOMP THE ELEPHANT IN THE OFFICE

Steven W. Vannoy and
Craig W. Ross

Wister & Willows, Publishers Inc.
Lakewood, Colorado

Wister & Willows, Publishers Inc.
3609 S. Wadsworth Boulevard, Suite 380
Lakewood, Colorado 80235

www.verusglobal.com

Library of Congress Control Number 2007930446
Stomp the elephant in the office: Put an end to the toxic
workplace, get more done – and be excited about work
again / by Steven W. Vannoy and Craig W. Ross

ISBN 978-0-9793768-0-1

Printed in Canada on acid-free paper.

Dedicated...

*...to the humble and accomplished leaders, at all levels,
who have taught us what leadership is about...*

*...to our parents, who through their devotion
have provided the most significant
life lessons and opportunities...*

*...and to those we do it all for: the families.
They are the heart of every person's leadership,
and the keeper of the world's future.*

ACKNOWLEDGMENTS

In the course of realizing dreams we have learned what those who have gone before us already understand: It is not where you go that makes life gratifying; it is who you get there with that makes it all worthwhile. The body of work in your hands is serving thousands of people around the world because of the dedication of special people.

We would like to thank the Verus Global family. To those who have and continue to work at the home office, along with the facilitators around the globe—thank you. Day in and day out, behind mountains of projects, through delayed flights and calendaring requests of the impossible, you excel. Your selfless acts and commitment to purpose inspire us.

In addition, there are individuals whom many people would call clients; we are honored to call them friends. These are people who, long before Verus Global came along, have dedicated their lives to making a difference through their leadership. We are in awe of the changes you are bringing to the planet and are grateful to be partnered with you in this important endeavor.

Included in the group above are individuals who took time to review and support this book. Your contributions have been mighty. Thank you for the wisdom you shared that brought this book to where it is today.

Of special note, we would like to thank our editors and designers, including Nancy Zellig, Allison St. Claire, Lisa Smith, Linda Parker, Dianne Nelson, and Karen Saunders. Your talents are rich; thank you for lending them to this project.

Through each day there are people close to us who practice important leadership qualities: acceptance, patience and an undying belief that the vision is possible. We are honored to walk this path with you. From Steve: Barb, Emmy, Ali, and Katie . . . from Craig: Amanda, Shea, Jolie and Lara . . . thank you for the gift of love and family that is unparalleled.

Contents

PROLOGUE

"The elephant in the room" is an American idiom, a popular phrase that implies there is inappropriate or distasteful information or behavior everyone is aware of—the elephant—but no one is talking about it or doing anything about it. As a result, the information or behavior cannot be dealt with, and the elephant cannot be evicted.

The elephant addressed in this book is the poor behaviors, attitudes and dysfunctional actions of individuals and teams that stop people from getting things done. This elephant robs people of excitement they once had for their work. *Stomp the Elephant in the Office* provides tools and methodologies to evict the elephant from the workplace and home. If the elephant is not evicted, the things you need to get done—your strategies—are crushed, money is lost, and lives are damaged.

The elephant need not exist. You can do something, starting now. You can be the one who leads and creates an elephant-free office.

The Proof:
Elephant Tracks in Your Organization

"I'm going to use a highly technical term," a VP recently said. "We suck at executing strategies."

He and his organization are not alone. In a study by Ernst & Young, 66 percent of corporate strategy is never executed. Some say the failure rate is even higher. Why aren't things getting done? And what can you do about it?

This is clear: How well people work together and how effective they are at their jobs—your work culture, in other words—determine the success of your organization's strategies. Everyone knows this, yet few people have the courage to talk about culture—and even fewer have the skill to do anything about it. "Culture" has become an elephant. Those who do create elephant-free workplaces deliver results that turn heads and change the face of their workplaces. How they do it is the essence of *Stomp the Elephant in the Office*.

Maybe some people do not take on their elephants because they do not know what to say or do. After all, no one goes to college and majors in "culture," and our fathers' generation labeled such talk as soft.

No wonder most leaders allow the elephant—the often unspoken truth about poor behaviors, attitudes and the inability to execute—to devour and destroy their organizational strategies. Organizations that do not eliminate their elephants harbor toxic cultures that eat every opportunity created.

The successful organizations and leaders identified in this book consider the effectiveness with which people work together as the mother of all strategies.

Rich Crawford is the global president for O-I, the largest glass producer in the world. He helped O-I Latin America to a number-one leadership position in most financial and operational KPIs (key performance indicators) in less than one year. This resulted in all-time record levels of earnings in 2006. Rich is a leader dedicated to creating elephant-free workplaces.

"I came into the Latin American job," he said, "knowing it would be complicated to manage a region that covered more than an entire continent. I couldn't leverage my style by being with them personally. As I put together my one-hundred-day plan for execution, this topped my list: immediately build an even stronger work culture and leadership team. Then, with them establish what is most important for the region." Rich continued, "I'm an engineer by trade. I've always believed that structure follows strategy. But neither one of those work if you don't have attitude and ownership—and that's culture."

How Big Is the Elephant in Your Office?

Take this quiz to determine the size of the big-eared beast in your office. True or False:

1. Sometimes you feel like your title should be changed to chief firefighter.

2. Too often meetings are counterproductive and waste time.

3. Commonly, top-down leadership approaches point out people's flaws and mistakes.

4. The high point for excitement comes at the end of the day as people walk out the door.

5. Productivity would increase if some colleagues called in sick.

6. Sometimes you find yourself thinking, "I work with idiots who mess everything up."

7. Too many people roll their eyes when they hear of the company's goal of being an employer of choice.

8. Some people suffer joint discomfort from pointing their fingers when mistakes happen.

9. Your organization has a greater understanding of what does not work vs. what does.

10. "That's not my job" is the mantra for some teams.

There are other signs that an elephant exists; however, if you answered in the affirmative to any of the above symptoms, things are not getting done around you. The moment your organization stomps this elephant, the people in your organization will become more aligned with their purpose and profitability will surge. The excitement for doing the work you do will rise. Proof of this is contained within these pages.

Who Is the Elephant's Keeper?

Getting the elephant out of the office is today's urgent organizational task. So, who is responsible for the elephant? Fingers have been pointed at your boss, the human resources department, organizational history and bad luck. Yet, like it or not, nearly every person holding this book knows that if you are part of a team, you influence the culture. You are responsible for the size of the elephant in your office. Regardless of our positions, we each influence culture; the elephant is everyone's business.

Stomp the Elephant in the Office is for people who want to lead—who want to make a difference—from where they are. It is for people who harbor the desire for high performance and excellence, who know that bottom-line results are a product of human results.

**These leaders understand
that a healthy, productive culture
is either dying or
being born and nurtured during
every interaction of every day.**

You May Recognize Yourself

You will recognize the leadership tools and methodologies we describe in this book because they are grounded in basic human behaviors. Yet, as we have observed over our combined fifty years of leadership work in various industries, only a small number of people consistently apply and leverage these universal truths.

When they do, they and the teams they work with outperform everyone around them. Those who disregard these truths, either consciously or unconsciously, sabotage their own best efforts and remain mired in mediocrity. Aaron Hilkemann, CEO of Duncan Aviation in Lincoln, Nebraska, concurs: "The tools Vannoy and Ross share may be common sense, but they are not commonly applied."

Because these tools have their roots in the choices each person makes every day, those who apply the tools described in *Stomp the Elephant in the Office* deliver greater results, many say immediately.

We and our team at Verus Global Inc. currently assist people in organizations on six continents—from CEOs to those working on the line; from small teams to Fortune 100 companies; from leaders in education and government to parent groups to those in the nonprofit sector. These people are mastering these tools and becoming better leaders. They are making greater contributions while building extraordinary workplaces, organizations, families and communities.

"By using these tools, our employees have rapidly become better leaders," said Roger Stortenbecker, chief development officer for Developmental Services of Nebraska Inc., a not-for-profit agency. "Not only are we better able to achieve the organization's mission to support persons with disabilities, but our employees are also taking these tools and concepts outside the workplace, enriching their families, schools and communities."

The Following People
Will Not Be Interested in This Book

People who favor a *results-at-any-cost* approach will not find this book appealing. While the pressures of the marketplace and Wall Street are real, so are the demands of human consciousness. In this book you will find an organizational approach that satisfies both. Numbers matter. So do the people who generate those numbers.

Results are an effect; people are the cause.

When people function in a way that develops and supports values and productive qualities and behaviors—the essence of culture—something startling happens: Effective decision making and strong execution of strategies are predetermined rather than demanded at the moment of need or after the fact. This values-based approach prepares individuals and organizations for whatever situations they encounter. And people become more excited about the work they do.

This natural, elephant-free approach—a Wellness Culture approach—is a process rather than the one-time or event-oriented strategy so often employed in traditional leadership. The leaders highlighted in this book demonstrate that when they use this method, engagement and motivation—buzzwords of the past decade—are no longer a hoped-for but often unrealized objective. Instead, they are the natural outcome. Organizations free themselves of deterrents, elephants and otherwise, to lead in their industry and in the marketplace.

We are honored to share the stories and best practices of those who are innovating and evolving the way successful leadership gets done.

The Leader Next Door

Many books have been written about the leadership and cultural practices of individuals and companies who are the darlings of Wall Street. These leaders and organizations, some of whom are featured in this book, deserve the recognition.

With *Stomp the Elephant in the Office*, however, we will explore something unique. We have discovered concepts and tools beyond those used by the traditionally celebrated leaders and companies. We examine countless unsung heroes who provide noteworthy leadership within organizations that some of you may not recognize.

These are people who live in neighborhoods like yours, regular people who quietly deliver outstanding results. Some of them work for organizations that are scratching their way into the marketplace. Others work for companies that are under severe financial stress or seem to be in chaos or afloat in a sea of toxicity. Yet these people are making a difference and producing amazing results for themselves and their immediate teams, proving to be an irreplaceable piece of their company's comeback strategy.

For example, in the following pages, you will read about a group within Ford Motor Company that, despite the parent organization's significant and very public struggles, is achieving what no one before them ever has. You will also learn what a select group of leaders at a carton manufacturing company in the Midwest, called Caraustar, is doing that allows them to cut out a piece of the pie in a market dominated by larger corporations.

Finally, some of the leaders highlighted in this book do not work for shareholders; some do not hold traditional positions of power. In the end, though, all of them have refined an approach to their jobs and lives that serves as a model for those who aspire to achieve and deliver their leadership best.

It is time to address the elephant in the office so people, purpose and profitability come into alignment. This book is devoted to giving you proven tools to move your leadership, culture and results forward now.

Part One

THE ELEPHANT-FREE WORKPLACE

Creating a Wellness Culture Where More Things Get Done

*The desire to fulfill our own potential
is as natural as wanting to breathe.*

*People in their natural state are motivated.
It is the job of every person within the culture
to create an environment that allows people
to nurture and build that inner motivation.*

CHAPTER 1

The Five Approaches To Dealing with The Elephant

Which Method Do You Use?

When it comes to culture and its development, organizations use one of five basic approaches.

1. *"There Is an Elephant in the Office" Approach.* Teamwork may be discussed and ropes may be climbed in these organizations, but the all-important "C" word—culture—remains whispered in the hallways. The elephant remains unmentioned, though it stands in the middle of the room munching on strategies and initiatives for lunch. Futile attempts to direct the culture through fix-it strategies such as policies, mandates and cascaded information lead to devastating results and the loss of human potential. These are often toxic places to work.

2. *The "Wish Management" Approach.* While people intuitively know what is right and wrong, they take few inten-

3

tional actions in these organizations because they do not know how to take them. Culture is talked about, but guessing, wishing and hoping are the primary strategies for creating an effective one. Hiring for talent with little regard for character is the norm in such companies. Inevitably, all these tactics lead to "You can't change people" being muttered over unsatisfactory spreadsheets.

3. *The "Cheerleader" Approach.* People in these organizations are exposed to motivational speakers, false praise, elaborate rewards and other gimmicks in an effort to externally motivate and engage them. Rhetoric rules, with trite clichés posted and then forgotten in a day. People are smart; they grow tired of such patently manipulative moves. They are left feeling disenfranchised while objectives are never fully realized. The true language of an effective culture remains foreign.

4. *The "People Are Our Priority" Approach.* These organizations have addressed the elephant, and thus enjoy fewer personnel issues. Culture, discussed openly within boardrooms, bathrooms and everywhere else, is the priority. Yet the workforce, while engaged and feeling good, remains unharnessed and unfocused, and strategies are poorly executed. Here, people are excited about *where* they work, but not the work they do.

That is because such organizations miss the point: Results are the priority. People and culture are the strategies to achieve the priority: to deliver results.

5. *The "Wellness Culture" Approach.* This approach, defined and highlighted in this book, creates a culture in

which the workforce is engaged and its actions are aligned with the organization's strategies and business objectives. These organizations consistently strengthen this link because they know that effective cultures are not a one-size-fits-all proposition. These groups have a common language that addresses individual and collective behaviors—everyone becomes more efficient. It is only in Wellness Cultures that individuals and their organizations realize their true potentials.

Mark Cicotello, vice president of human resources for the Heska Corporation, located in Loveland, Colorado, has seen his company face numerous challenges and still work its way to profitability. He describes the fifth approach to dealing with the elephant this way: "The Wellness Culture approach is not just about helping people be great and creating an exceptional culture. It's about doing both those things in a focused manner. It's about being great and having a culture *aligned* with your strategies and business model. This is the difference that makes us exceptional."

CHAPTER 2

When the Elephant Does Not Exist

How a Culture Delivers Profits

Imagine you are in charge. For a moment, picture yourself as the decision maker for an organization that is preparing to manufacture a new vehicle. You are a leader and a part of an international company that has been in severe trouble; tens of thousands of people are losing jobs because your company has lost market share to foreign automakers. Quality issues and customer appeal are significant topics in many meetings.

Now imagine that you are responsible for the new vehicle launch. The eyes of your company, the entire automotive world, the local community and legions of longtime customers are on you. The stakes are high. What is your plan? Where do you start?

Most leaders in this situation would go with what they know. They would do business—they would lead—the way they have always done it. Would you?

Those responsible for the new Ford Fusion, Mercury Milan, and Lincoln Zephyr did not. As a result, they achieved unprecedented success. According to Michael Collins, in his article "Fusion, Milan, Zephyr Score Best Start-up Quality Ever" (*Outstanding News*, Oct. 25, 2006), "Ford corporate research shows that the three vehicles had the best quality showing of any vehicle in Ford's long history. They outpaced segment leaders, Toyota Camry and Honda Accord."

The leaders of this team within the global auto giant did not achieve these results easily; they achieved them *differently*.

Can You and Your Team Deliver When You Most Need To?

The leadership responsibilities for a vehicle launch are extraordinary. The pressures are immeasurable. Hundreds of people invest years in developing the new automobile. Then thousands of people—who have not worked together before— gather to assemble the thousands of parts necessary to make a car that has never been built before. Understandably, vehicle launches are traditionally not a feel-good experience; veterans report health problems, high employee turnover, ill will toward colleagues and company, and a severe strain on family life.

So where did this successful Ford leadership team begin? "We knew we had to get upstream and start building leadership capacity well before the first car came off the line," said Rick Popp, then the director of human resources for Ford of Mexico. "Also, while the site already had a healthy culture, everyone wanted to take it to a new level. The specific leadership tools discussed in this book allowed us to make that happen."

"We are proud of the Wellness Culture we've developed here," said José Islas, the plant manager at Hermosillo, the location of the massive launch. Years ago, however, José may have taken a different approach. He is a large man with a booming voice, and when he walks into the room there is no doubt who is in charge.

Three years before the new vehicle launch, at the end of a Wellness Culture training, José shared with everyone his commitment to begin serving his people in a forward-focused way. This proclamation turned heads; until then the traditional approach had supported a strategy of intimidation, including raising voices, making threats and demands, and minimizing the value each person brought to the process.

Two years later, we had a conversation with José. "I am very busy preparing," he said.

"Preparing for what?" we asked.

"We have 120 people from the United States coming to visit and learn from us."

"That's quite an honor. Why are they visiting you?"

"When you are at the top of the hill, people want to know what you're doing," he said with an uncomfortable laugh. Although José is very proud of his plant, he is not the type to boast about the plant's success.

"What areas are you at the top of the hill in?"

"We are the #1 plant in North America. We're Best in Class [vehicle type, in and out of Ford]. We're first in cost, and we're first in quality. We've got safety covered. We deliver."

"José, what would you attribute those successes to?"

"The culture we've been developing for the last couple of years accounts for eighty percent of the success we're having here. It's no secret: The only difference is people. You can be great in technology, you can be great in processes and everything else, but the difference maker is the people.

"When I conduct my skip-level meetings [meetings with employees he does not directly interact with], I get feedback that we are communicating much better and creating more trust. Our whole group is more open to feedback. And we're much better at providing recognition of others. People are starting to feel better!"

Then, foreseeing the stresses of the impending launch that was over a year away, José added, "Problems will still come. But how we deal with those problems will make all the difference."

The problems did come. Immediately after the start of the launch, one of the largest parts suppliers filed for bankruptcy. The supplier was in chaos; delayed and incomplete deliveries put the entire operation at risk. Ford of Mexico immediately sent in a group of their own leaders to stabilize the situation. The delays in production and other losses could have been devastating, yet this Ford team did not falter. Why?

"Our plan worked," said Louise Goeser, CEO of Ford of Mexico. "From the start, we intentionally developed the people. All supervisors at the site received training in Wellness Culture in order to (1) be prepared to handle the high stress of the launch in a healthy way; (2) establish healthy organizational behaviors with a new working pattern, six days per week; (3) provide leadership tools to continually develop culture, improve relationships and improve leadership behaviors; and (4) build on a 'One Team' concept with actual tools."

"With hundreds of people coming to our location from other Ford sites, along with hiring thousands of new employees, we made it a priority to build on the culture we've worked so hard to achieve," said Fausto Flores, manager of human resources for the Hermosillo plant. By focusing on the Wellness Culture, they positively influenced those partnering with them to the point that, as Flores said, "We accelerated our results, and got closer as a team."

Stellar results continue to pour in. The team exceeded their warranty targets by 45 percent, bettered their cost targets, and bested their target TGW (Things Gone Wrong) score. The results sit among the industry's best.

These Ford vehicles continue to gain international attention, including prestigious ratings and awards from JD Power and the cover story of *Consumer Reports* magazine (October 2006), among others.

Visitors to the launch site often ask, "What are the top reasons for the excellent quality and overall success?" Felix Guillen, director of manufacturing operations at Ford of Mexico, replies, "You can take the five or six best practices and replicate them elsewhere, and still not have the same results if the alignment of culture, behaviors, competencies, values and management mindset are not at the same level. The recipe is—and is not—simple."

 What recipe are you and your organization using to align people with your strategies and purpose for doing business?

CHAPTER 3

What an Elephant-Free Workplace Looks Like

The Three Pillars of a Wellness Culture

A Wellness Culture occurs when any group of people is free of elephants. This sort of culture aligns people, purpose and profitability, and is built on three fundamental pillars:

1. A group of people committed to fostering the development of healthy individuals, teams and systems proactively *rather than* trying to fix people and problems reactively.

2. An environment that allows people to be who they truly want to be—to be great—*rather than* stifling their natural motivation to contribute fully.

3. A group of people on a quest to understand what is working *rather than* what is not working, to focus on solutions and strengths *rather than* on problems and weaknesses, and to find the value in what is happening *rather than* concentrating on who or what is to blame.

Most people intuitively know when they are operating in such a culture—and when they are not. Here are just a few of the ways people describe being in an elephant-free workplace:

- "We can tell the truth about issues that we're facing."

- "Everyone is on the same page."

- "You can feel momentum and energy."

- "Meetings are fewer and shorter."

- "We get work done faster."

- "Our strategies work so we get the results we wanted."

- "We're excited about our opportunities."

By identifying and understanding the elephant in the office—the poor behaviors, negative attitudes and dysfunctional actions that impede progress—organizations begin the process of getting rid of it. They can then focus on developing and leveraging their culture for greater results beyond those mentioned above.

What have you done to permanently eradicate elephants from your office? Your answer reveals your organization's aptitude for using the most important and effective business strategy available.

You Have a Unique Opportunity

The tools highlighted in this book are proven and easy to apply. Unfortunately, day-to-day work in any field is not a linear practice. Even with the best planning, opportunities to lead and to make an impact on the culture occur randomly in any person's day.

Given that randomness, it is important to explore what many people consider the most important factor in building a Wellness Culture: the Humanity Factor. It is this factor that people use as they encounter the countless challenges and issues they face every day. It is this factor that assists them in being the people they have always known they can be.

Angie Paccione is a former Colorado state representative. She said, "The Wellness Culture approach puts a structure around the values I have. This means that I'm able to live out of and leverage those values much more consistently."

Moving Forward with the Humanity Factor as a Foundation

We ask that you take an unusual action right now. We invite you to skip to the final part of this book, part eight, The Humanity Factor, which begins on page 295, and read it next. Part eight does not reveal a destination that effective leaders strive toward. It does describe an approach that effective leaders like Angie Paccione and others *begin* with.

The Humanity Factor is an understanding that wellness leaders—leaders in Wellness Cultures—manifest in everything they do. It not only determines the success these leaders have in applying the tools shared in this book, it also determines the level of satisfaction they receive from leading.

So, please mark this page so you can easily return to it after you have finished part eight. Again, it begins on page 295.

Welcome back. The concepts in part eight inject value into everything else you will read from here on, adding meaning and importance far beyond the ordinary. The Humanity Factor amplifies our effectiveness as leaders. It raises the standard for our interactions with others and the approach to building a healthy, productive culture. It shapes the results we deliver. The Humanity Factor allows a leader to enter into a partnership with others that is becoming increasingly rare in an increasingly impersonal world. This partnership is a bond that serves as the glue of a Wellness Culture.

As you think of the leaders you have admired most, under what circumstances have you seen them demonstrate the Humanity Factor? How does this factor align with your values?

CHAPTER 4

When the Elephant Is Ignored: The Toxic "Fix-It" Culture

You Know You Have a Toxic Culture When . . .

We will examine, define and show examples of each Wellness Culture pillar in the next three chapters. But first, let us take a closer look at what a Wellness Culture is—and is not.

A friend described the following experience. Unfortunately, meetings such as this take place with great frequency around the world. In this and in other case studies to follow, names have been changed but the essence of the stories remains.

A Case Study:
We Are Experts at Knowing Why We Are Failures

The last person to enter the conference room brought everyone to attention. He slapped a handful of file folders on the table, crossed his arms and stared at

17

the team. No one moved except for Bridget, who sighed and rolled her eyes.

"I thought we had this taken care of," Doug said, as he unfolded his arms and leaned forward on the table. "But apparently I was wrong."

Everyone in the room knew this routine, but that did not make it any easier. Pens and fingernails suddenly demanded inspection.

"We set our goals and each of you determined your tasks, but you couldn't make that work. So we walked you through what was necessary—what each one of you was supposed to do—and you still couldn't get it right."

He stood, yanked at his collar and crossed his arms again. "So we did an off-site, played with ropes for a while, and made promises to each other like little kids in a sandbox." He swiped at a folder, sending it and its contents fluttering into the corner.

"And here we sit, auditioning for *Dumb and Dumber*.

"Apparently you can't see it, so let me lift the fog for you." He turned and looked directly at the man immediately to his left, his eyes blinking rapidly behind his glasses. "We're over budget—and not by a little bit."

He paused, allowing his words to sink in as he turned his gaze to the sharply dressed VP of marketing four chairs down on his right. "We're six months away from launch, but I don't think you'd be ready if you had six years."

Finally, he snapped his glare toward Bridget, who was looking at him with a venomous smile. "And inventory is so screwed up, we don't know if we're coming or going."

He slumped to his seat. "People, *please*," he said, his hands stretched in supplication, "what's it going to take?"

Bridget did not waste any time. "That's easy, Doug."
Fake smile intact, she swiveled to stare at the man across
from her. "We just need an accurate forecast. If I get
that, I'll have inventory squared away."

The lob was too well placed for her counterpart to
miss. "Is it that easy, Bridget?" His finger swept the
room. "My forecast has been as good as it can be, given
the inconsistent feedback I get from marketing, sales and
production!"

An uncomfortable pause blanketed the room as
everyone cautiously looked toward the head of the table.
Doug shrugged his shoulders. He was not letting them
off the hook.

More silence. Monica from human resources finally
spoke up. "Is it any wonder we're getting killed in our
employee satisfaction surveys? Look at how we're act
ing. We need to hear what team members are thinking
and talk about how we're operating," she said.

"Well, that's not what I want to talk about," Doug
cut in. "We're paying these people to work. They can
leave the thinking to us. What I want to talk about is
getting results!" He slammed his fist on the table to
punctuate his rant. As he opened his mouth to continue,
he paused when he noticed a note being passed from one
person to the next at the far end of the table.

"Do you kids mind letting me in on the secret?" He
put his hand out, demanding the note.

When the small piece of paper reached the head of
the table, Doug unfolded it and read:

"WE'RE EXPERTS AT KNOWING WHY
WE'RE FAILURES. WE DON'T HAVE A
CLUE ABOUT HOW TO BE SUCCESSFUL."

"What is that supposed to mean?" he asked through
gritted teeth.

The Fix-It Approach

Many of us have experienced organizational cultures lost in destructive fix-it cycles. Instead of developing functioning relationships and healthy systems up front, these organizations wait for unsatisfactory outcomes and then spend much of their time and resources trying to fix people, teams and problems after the fact. The typical cycle looks like this:

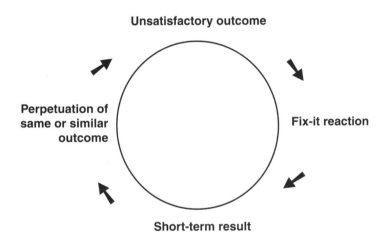

The destructive forces of a fix-it culture stand in contrast to the Wellness Culture approach:

- Organizations pay to do a job twice—instead of creating a Wellness Culture that aligns people and purpose so things are done right the first time.

- Supervisors, who see themselves as the experts, fill their to-do lists with items to tell their teams—rather than helping team members develop behaviors so they can think for themselves.

- Managers implement countless policies and procedures to catch slackers—instead of establishing a foundation of trust in the first place.

- Teams analyze and discuss why projects fail—instead of deciding what is necessary for them to succeed.

- Leaders notice and announce when employees are not performing well—rather than noticing and announcing when they are achieving.

- Managers lament and blame disengaged employees—instead of taking responsibility for behavior outcomes the same way they do for business outcomes.

- Companies give lip service to diversity of experience, thoughts and ideas—rather than leveraging these naturally occurring resources.

- Organizations have no time for fun and celebration ("Hey, we've got problems to focus on!")—instead of encouraging such practices to ensure the priceless resources of pride and confidence.

Companies that are trampled by the elephant in the fix-it mentality hire talented young guns and experienced old pros. Then, with the intention of building future leaders, they instead train followers and firefighters who manage by crisis. The cumulative effect of person after person operating this way guarantees and perpetuates a downward, toxic cycle.

**What kind of results do fix-it cultures produce?
A sad return on investments, poor use of
resources, propped-up bottom lines,
embarrassing public relations—
and bleeding morale.**

Are People Really a
Company's Greatest Asset?

The Gallup Institute of Research reported that 55 percent of American workers are disengaged in their jobs. "Imagine what it means to the bottom line when over half of your workforce doesn't want to be at work," said one mid-level manager.

But it gets worse for the average company: An additional 17 percent of workers are *actively* disengaged. "In other words," continued the manager, "these companies would be better off if these people did not show up for work. These employees are costing the company more than they are being paid."

These statistics shoot down the platitude, "Our people are our greatest asset." This cannot be the case if 72 percent of employees are disengaged. The mantra should read: "Our people are our greatest asset *when we have an elephant-free workplace.*"

People who have their sights set on a Wellness Culture leverage their efforts more effectively than those who are merely attempting to create greater engagement in their workforce. Having people awake at work does not get the results needed.

A Wellness Culture creates ownership:
a step above buy-in and two steps
beyond engagement. Ownership leads to
long-term execution and results.

People take ownership when organizations and their leaders spend less time trying to fix people and problems and more time honoring employees' motivations and skills and connecting them to clear goals, execution plans and results. In other words, people take ownership when a Wellness Culture exists. Take, for example, what Felix Guillen of Ford Mexico has found:

"Here is a glimpse of what a Wellness Culture looks like for us.

"While walking the floor of the supplier's plant, I asked the young foreman providing the tour, 'How much do you like this company?'

"He smiled and said, 'I like it a lot.'

"'Why?'

"'Well, they care about people,' he answered.

"'And how do you know? How do you measure that?'

"He didn't have an answer. His face went blank as he walked away, but in fifteen minutes he was back.

"'I have an answer for you,' he said. He patted his chest with both hands and said, 'Look at me! I'm how you measure it!'"

CHAPTER 5

Creating an Elephant-Free Workplace: Wellness Culture Pillar #1

What this pillar looks like: A group of people committed to fostering the development of healthy individuals, teams and systems proactively rather than trying to fix people and problems reactively.

To achieve results, most companies invest in strategies that require significant organizational management and process deployment—all costly ventures. Sound business strategies are a must, but without the proactive element of this first Wellness Culture component, the strategies are likely to fail.

The primary reason? Today's market often shifts faster than you can read this chapter; organizations that emphasize strategy over people cannot adapt quickly *because the people responsible for the work are not driving the change.* These companies cannot keep pace in a mobile market and are doomed to a pattern of cutting losses as they revise game plan after game plan. Meanwhile, their employees grow increasingly tired of the pattern and check out. Conversely, organizations that emphasize strategy *with* culture can change quickly—*because people adapt more quickly than systems.*

Mark Cicotello of Heska Corporation said, "Culture eats strategy for lunch. Either you become the architect of your culture or it becomes the architect and manages you."

Policies and Rules: Nurturing the Elephant in the Office

Steven Vannoy[1]: "On a recent business trip from Frankfurt, Germany, back to Denver, I had a layover in Chicago. After multiple gate changes, airline errors and miscommunications, I was eight hours late arriving in Denver.

"I shared my disappointment with a gate agent. The agent's response was shocking: 'We're not worried about losing your business, because no other airline can do any better. If we lose your business, we'll just trade you for the customers our competition is losing.'

"Sub-par customer service is appalling. Yet when some organizations discover poor customer service within their ranks, their managers inadvertently perpetuate the very behavior they want to eliminate.

"Not two weeks after the experience with the gate agent, I had an in-flight conversation with a middle manager from the same airline. I told her about my experience.

"She shook her head and related how the company had made repeated efforts to 'stop employees from offending customers.' She said, 'In fact, right now we're implementing

---

[1] Occasionally we will interrupt the narrative voice used throughout most of this book to share an experience or insight in first person. When this happens we will make sure it is clear which one of us is speaking.

additional accountability policies and measures.' She added that she would like to see tighter discipline and controls, and she lamented the state of the employee base today."

Did you catch it? This type of reaction breeds the very behavior it is designed to eliminate. This middle manager's abusive approach to getting results ignores and enrages the elephant in her office; her outdated approach of whipping the elephant characterizes slow-moving leaders, teams and companies that operate in a fix-it culture.

Organizations that foster such cultures find it nearly impossible for their teams to successfully execute strategies or sustain a competitive advantage in their market. They have unsuccessfully wagered the achievement of their business objectives on the idea that productivity and excellence in any area can be forced. These futile attempts to control people cost organizations focus, time and money. They become handcuffed by their own cultures because employees are *further out of alignment* with organizational strategies and objectives.

Guidance from leaders about what is important and necessary regarding procedures and standards is critical. Policies involving health and safety are a must. In a Wellness Culture, everyone owns these policies and leverages them for greater results.

Policies should empower, not disable.

Sadly, overbearing policies are the backbone of many toxic cultures. When policies and rules exceed their ability and intention to support people, they are like weeds in a garden—choking life and reducing the fruit harvest.

Savvy leaders ask, "Does the policy align us with our strategies, business objectives and model of doing business?" These people know that every policy influences and potentially alters the culture, so they are extra careful to consider the ramifications.

"Cultureship"—A Leader's Priority

To what extent do you possess the ability to lead the culture of your organization? Wellness leaders make this their number-one priority because they know their organization must sail successfully through a sea of strategies. Developing people, relationships and systems proactively ensures that resources are used effectively.

Numerous people who have proven themselves effective at cultureship have focused on building this pillar of a Wellness Culture and report that such an approach is five to twenty-five times more cost effective as a way of doing business. Savings show up in numerous areas: improved production efficiencies; fewer product recalls; greater employee retention and loyalty; positive public relations; and increased customer satisfaction.

When resources are no longer tied up in attempts to fix yesterday's problems and put out fires, they can be used to be proactive, which establishes competitive advantages. It is then that companies start to distinguish themselves from their competitors.

The three pillars of a Wellness Culture serve as blueprints for building an elephant-free zone that is a healthy, productive culture in both the workplace and family. Developing these three pillars does not cost a dime. Developing them does not require a reorganization, a capital investment or a buyout. What it does require is greater management of self, and effectiveness while interacting with others. This is leadership.

CHAPTER 6

Creating an Elephant-Free Workplace: Wellness Culture Pillar #2

What this pillar looks like: An environment that allows people to be who they truly want to be to be great—rather than stifling their natural motivation to contribute fully.

This pillar is cemented in a powerful understanding that every person wants to be great, that each of us wants to know that we matter. Consider that every person on the planet wants to achieve objectives, wants to be a member of an outstanding team that delivers stellar results. While some people may have received a lifetime of negative messages that they do not have significant potential or abilities, consider that even these people harbor a desire for greatness, that deep inside resides a need to be understood.

The desire to fulfill our own potential is as natural as wanting to breathe.

29

A Case Study:
A Celebrated Business Leader's Retirement Speech

Forty-two years ago, I received my first management position. I was responsible for leading twelve people. Fresh out of college, I was ready to change the world. Fortunately, I learned something early that changed everything for me. If I hadn't learned this lesson, I wouldn't be the person who is standing in front of you today.

Thirty years ago, a man named Stan was the first to be honored with the "Cubicle with a View" worksite that some of you have since been distinguished with. He deserved more than that cubicle. When Stan said good-bye to our company, I bought him dinner. If I had known then what I know now, I would have bought him more than that. For it was Stan who gave me the greatest leadership lesson I would ever learn.

When I became Stan's boss, I was determined to prove to my supervisors that they had promoted the right person to double productivity. They had warned me about Stan. If I didn't get him up to speed quickly, then we would both be escorted out the door. They called him Dino, short for dinosaur. Not only his shirts and ties but his methodologies and actions were also outdated. "Clean house" is what they told me when I signed the contract.

My second day on the job, I called Stan into my windowless office. I knew little about the old man—had hardly even heard him talk. Frankly, I suspected the meeting would last two minutes and then my "Stan problem" would be over.

He stood in front of my desk and seemed to find something important about his shoes to stare at. As I looked at him, I felt my stomach tighten. What was I doing sitting in this chair? This man in front of me seemed three times my age. With this, I forgot the words I had prepared. Suddenly confused, I asked him a question. "How many years have you been with us?"

"Thirty-one," he responded.

I admit it: I froze. This man had more years of experience than I had years alive, and I was responsible for him. Unexpectedly, he fascinated me.

"What was it like when you started here?" I asked him.

He didn't answer. He just kept looking down at his shoes. I thought about retreating to the few words I could remember from my speech, but something about this guy gave me pause.

I got up from my seat and leaned against the corner of my desk. "Really, Stan," I said, "what was it like here?"

He looked at me for a second, and I thought I saw a grin. The words came gently and firmly, and not one was wasted. It was quickly apparent that we were opening a vault that had been closed for years. Five minutes into his reflections, I coyly reached for my pen. Ten minutes after that I couldn't have cared less that he knew his boss was taking copious notes.

With smiles and frowns, he shared stories about how this department had once set the standard for the company. He talked about the day when people from this department would go on to high-level positions—but how he stayed because he liked the work.

I peppered him with questions: "What were they trying to achieve?" "How did they do that?"

He had answers to everything I threw at him, including the last question I asked nearly an hour after we'd begun. It was this question that changed who I am as a leader. "Stan," I said, and then paused. "If you were in my shoes, what would you do with this department?"

It's probably not a surprise to you that he looked at his shoes again. I guess he felt it would be disrespectful for him to answer this one. But after hearing all the wisdom contained in the vault of his experiences, I knew I had to have the answer to this last question. I asked him again, "Stan, what would you do?"

He lifted his head and told me. And I wrote down every word.

You already know that Stan's action plan wasn't what changed everything for me. It's the fact that Stan *had* an action plan that changed me. From that day forward, Stan and every man and woman on that team became my partner. Within a month we exceeded our six-month goal. We really started turning some heads.

When I got promoted upstairs, I wanted to take Stan with me, but he declined. He said he had less than a year before retirement and didn't want the hassle of moving his desk. But I knew it was something else: Stan didn't define "greatness" with the word "upstairs." Stan's greatness included words like "pride," "integrity," and "excellence." Yet even with his incredible determination, over time this company was able to force him to lock his greatness away. We're lucky he didn't throw away the key.

I made Stan move his desk anyhow. We created the Cubicle with a View worksite, and he was the first honoree. He was awfully proud of that site.

After retirement, he and his wife moved to Arizona. I got a few letters from him, but we've since fallen out of touch. But I haven't lost track of what he taught me— and how he changed me. If I had managed Stan the way I'd been taught to manage, I wouldn't be in front of you today.

Stan taught me that leadership has nothing to do with being the boss and everything to do with opening the vaults of greatness that everyone has within them.

From the day Stan stood in front of my desk, I moved forward assuming there was a Stan inside each of us. And that has changed everything.

I appreciate the recognition you are giving me today. I love this company, who we are, and who we serve. But you should know that by honoring me you are really honoring yourselves. For I have done nothing but allow you to do what it is you know you can do.

Welcome to Your Marriage. Now, Be a Jerk.

No one enters a marriage wanting it to fail. Similarly, most of us bring a high level of commitment to the workplace. It would be difficult to find one person who arrived for his first day on the job and thought, "I can't wait to mess things up and make life miserable for everyone! They're going to write policies because of me."

Yet too many people start new positions on a natural roll, excited about their work, imagining the possibilities—just as in a marriage—only to have this enthusiasm derailed by two conditions: (1) the people and culture around them; and (2) their inability to lead themselves.

How big is the elephant in this case? In nearly 85 percent of companies, employees' morale sharply declines after their first six months and continues to deteriorate in the years that follow. This finding is based on surveys, conducted by Sirota Survey Intelligence, of nearly 1.2 million employees at fifty-two primarily Fortune 1000 companies, from 2001 through

2004 ("Why Your Employees Are Losing Motivation," by Sirota, Mischkind, and Meltzer, *HBSWK*, April 2006).

What does it cost when people enter an organization and over time lose their desire to be great? To do their best work? Like world-class body builders once sculpted with muscle, these organizations see their muscle atrophy to fat. They require the same number of calories to survive but are unable to deliver the same results.

Do you want further proof that people want to be great? If so, answer this question: Do *you* want to be great?

We ask thousands of people around the world this question and, without fail, all hands go up in agreement.

Then we inquire: If we asked the same question of your colleagues, supervisors, direct reports, family members—everyone else in your life—how many hands would go up?

"All of them" is always the reply.

We also ask: "How many of you want to be average? Do marginal work? Be part of a mediocre team? Be a person who can't get things done?" No hand has ever been raised in response to these queries.

Companies around the world have strengthened this pillar of their Wellness Culture. Juan Pablo Ortiz Tirado Kelly, a leader in a large bank in Mexico, reveals an important result that comes from developing this pillar. He says, "One of the most important outcomes of our developing a Wellness Culture is the increase in our employee retention."

With this important element of a Wellness Culture—allowing people to be great—employees retain their "first day freshness." Years into their employment, they carry the same level of motivation and enthusiasm as they did their first day on the job because they do not have elephants in the office squeezing the greatness out of them. Their companies are truly employee-owned companies.

The Greatness People Want

The type of greatness we are describing does not involve spotlights or headlines; the being great that everyone desires has no ego. It is about feeling good; it is about living life on a roll; it's about handling the difficult circumstances in your life in a healthy way. More than anything else, it is about making a meaningful difference in our world.

You have already read about the Humanity Factor discussed in the last part of this book. When that factor is present, people care enough about other human beings to influence all their interactions with others. The Humanity Factor is an element—some say an outcome—of a person's natural desire to be great.

Knowing that people want to be great alters how we interact with others. The Humanity Factor is how we demonstrate our desire to be great as we all lead.

The essence of wanting to be great means being a part of something special, contributing fully, and knowing you matter. The Humanity Factor is all of that and more for influential people: It means they want to make a difference in the lives of everyone they come into contact with throughout the day.

For a woman named Susan, who works at a leading contact lens company, the use of this factor resulted in something she coveted. "I was struggling with the lack of balance in my life. I felt like I was putting a lot into work but was not getting a lot back. Because we have changed how we are showing up for work, the workplace has changed. I'm now getting more from work and consequently I feel more balance. For the most part it's not about the calendar. There's never going to be enough time. So it has to be about meaning. If you're adding meaning to your life then what you do affects you and others."

The strength of a culture is revealed by how effectively people in that culture interact with one another. When used, the Humanity Factor instantly gives organizational cultures an unshakeable foundation. As such an approach becomes a team's or a family's DNA, an unspoken agreement guarantees that the sum of the parts will be greater than the whole.

Trying to Motivate Your Team Is Insulting

When person A does not think person B wants to be great, person A often defaults to a belief that he[2] must *give* person B greatness. In other words, person A believes *he* must motivate B. This is the cheerleader or fix-it approach to developing a culture.

Jim Collins, in his book *Good to Great: Why Some Companies Make the Leap . . . And Others Don't* (Random House, 2001), presents research supporting the thesis that trying to motivate other people is a potentially costly mistake. The most frequently used motivational techniques are external and are applied with the intention of trying to *change* someone else. In fact, many motivational strategies *"de*-motivate" people. These strategies create followers who depend on external motivation, waste leaders' time by adding another task, and subtly send the insult that the employee is *not* motivated and needs fixing.

---

[2] We want to be gender sensitive. Advance readers of early drafts appreciated our first efforts to switch between "she" and "he," but found it slowed them down. With all respect to the women we have met, listened to, and worked with, we have decided to use the generic pronoun "he" uniformly throughout this book.

**People in their natural state are motivated.
It is the job of every person within the culture to
create an environment that allows people to
nurture and build that inner motivation.**

Surprisingly, even with research that proves otherwise, a majority of people continue to ask how they can better motivate others. Conversely, those leaders who have made the paradigm shift to the Wellness Culture approach understand that trying to *externally* move someone to do something is the "hamster in the wheel" approach. No wonder leaders who try to motivate others report they feel as if they are futilely spinning their wheels.

What Do People Want to Be Paid For?

As one supervisor told us, "The answer to what people want to be paid for is so obvious that most of us have conditioned ourselves not to see it anymore." Those who do see it truly lead and are a part of an inspired workforce.

What happens in an organization, a community or a nation when people have the opportunity to perform tasks they know will make a difference? Motivation and engagement become non-issues, while "what's possible" becomes a reality.

"Understanding that people want to be great has altered how I interact with others," said a director of operations at a manufacturing plant in Utah. "Consequently, it has altered how people respond to me. This simple truth has provided me with an immediate leadership upgrade." No one reading this book joined an organization with the intention of being average. None of us dreamed about being on a mediocre team, and none of us are content just taking up space on the planet. Most of us accepted responsibility with the desire to make an impact, to be part of a great team, to contribute to a better world.

Wellness leaders understand that everyone wants this chance; everyone wants to make a difference. This is what people want to get paid for. Effective leaders create elephant-free environments in their workplaces and homes to allow people to do just that.

Rich Crawford saw this firsthand within the first year of developing his team at O-I. "What we've discovered now, through this process of building a culture that drives our strategies, is how much our people care. They are more motivated than I ever imagined. And we got this way without adding any additional incentives." Obviously proud of the group, he added, "These guys really have this in their blood. They are more focused on serving and finding ways to develop people." He smiled. "It was a good group before. Now it's a great group."

Watch what happens—to capabilities, to trust and rapport, to the creation of new ideas, and to the way people rise to expectations—as the individuals in your organization begin to operate with the understanding that they are not the only ones who want to be great.

A controller at a Fortune 100 company said, "This concept works well by cutting to the core of understanding others' motivations. Understanding their view of the path to greatness and how our paths may converge has powerful implications that can be leveraged for everyone's benefit as well as for the success of the team."

When individuals within a common culture see that every person in every cubicle, in every position, in every meeting has the same desire, they find common ground.

This means alignment accelerates. Not just alignment of people—but alignment of people with the organization's purpose. Nothing beats aligning people, purpose and profitability.

CHAPTER 7

Creating an Elephant-Free Workplace: Wellness Culture Pillar #3

What this pillar looks like: A group of people on a quest to understand what is working rather than what is not working, to focus on solutions and strengths rather than on problems and weaknesses, and to find the value in what is happening rather than concentrating on who or what is to blame.

Elephant-free environments consist of people who are conscious of the direction and flow of human energy. They know their focus determines the direction in which they and those around them will move.

What happens when a group of people operate with the understanding that the quality and success of their experience depends on what they build rather than what they fix, how they view and communicate with one another, and what they focus on?

"What we've accomplished by building our Wellness Culture is nothing short of staggering," said David, a proactive leader within a Fortune 100 company.

"At one point our division was $450 million in the hole; last year we lost $200 million, and this year we're going to make money. Once there was finger pointing, an attitude of 'that's not the way we do it around here,' and leading only by doing. Now we use a common language. People are working together; they're singing the same tune. Our efforts to develop a Wellness Culture have everything to do with the results we're getting."

Your Culture's Operating System

What are the beliefs and behaviors that drive your culture? Moment after moment, leaders make statements and take actions that impel those around them either backward or forward. An organization's cultural operating system determines how these moments are managed, whether the office elephant is eradicated, and whether people, purpose and profitability are aligned.

Imagine working for a company that insists on using the traditional top-down approach where leaders attempt to *control* a culture rather than *develop* it. Such situations have aptly been described as toxic.

Imagine working for such a company and *still* waking up each morning and following through with the intention of building a Wellness Culture.

We are honored to work with such people, as you are honored to work next to them. These are the leaders without titles of influence, leaders who, even in the midst of extreme negativity, quietly create an oasis around them, a Wellness Culture that serves those who are lucky to be on the same team or in the same department. Often organizations do not know these subcultures exist directly under the feet of the elephant.

They simply know that in these places, strategies are executed and objectives achieved.

Consider the possibility that with increased awareness of the role a Wellness Culture plays in organizational success, numerous companies will make priceless discoveries simply by looking closely at themselves.

The Elephant-Free Home: Where the Most Important Leadership Work Occurs

Is the elephant in the office following you home? Wellness leaders know that business makes up only one element of our society. What impact would constructing a Wellness Culture have on a family? A religious institution? Our educational system? Government offices? The community as a whole? Are you making the difference you want to make everywhere you go? Or is your family simply getting your leftovers?

A man named Andy described a way he was able to make a positive difference in an organization's culture. "In my neighborhood association, the maintenance committee and beautification committee were at each others' throats. Beautification actions created more work for the overworked maintenance team; maintenance objections were an obstacle to beautification efforts. The situation was getting to be very personal.

"We called a joint meeting of the two committees. Before any business discussion or debate started, I asked everyone to identify three things they love about

(continued on next page)

**The Elephant-Free Home: Where the
Most Important Leadership Work Occurs**
(continued)

our community and to include at least one positive statement about one of the other committee members. We
shared everyone's responses and concluded that we all
value the same things. This restored trust. The committees agreed to merge budgets and have a common set
of objectives."

"My vision for a Wellness Culture is that it goes beyond our office, that it transcends the walls around us,"
said Marcos de Oliveira, while president of Ford of Mexico (he's now president of Ford Brazil). "This Wellness
Culture work affects me personally and my family. It has
the power to make Ford of Mexico an even better organization and also to make Mexico a better country."

Elephants have no boundaries. They are not con-
fined to offices. Likewise, wellness leadership has no
boundaries.

Part Two

GETTING INTO THE ELEPHANT REMOVAL BUSINESS BY BREAKING LEADERSHIP LOCK

The most important strategy an organization can develop is the strategy that determines how people lead others and themselves.

CHAPTER 8

Leadership Lock

What If What We Have Learned About Leadership Is Wrong?

People around the world are searching for the breakthrough innovation or secret strategy that will propel their organizations to the top. But what if the innovation that is needed most is in the leadership they display?

The most important strategy an organization can develop is the strategy that determines how people lead others and themselves.

There is ample evidence that a more effective way to lead is needed—bankruptcy, employee turnover, poor quality and loss of market share are just a few symptoms. Consider the possibility that the most dramatic way everyone can move their organizations, their communities and their families forward is to measurably improve how they lead.

45

What if some of us are approaching our work backwards? What if our attempts to set guidelines are actually confusing people, our efforts to motivate people are leaving them disenchanted and disengaged, and our endeavors to bring about change are solidifying resistance? What if the reason our teams, organizations and families are not moving forward is not because of them—but because of us? This is Leadership Lock: the gap between what is being achieved and what is possible.

Perhaps there is a gap between what we know and what we do, between the principles we value and the way we act. This gap may mark the difference between a dysfunctional team and an unbeatable team, between a family that lives with hurt and a family that lives its dreams.

The key to unlocking leadership is to innovate the leadership strategies we use.

A Case Study:
Michael's Leadership Lock

"It never ends," Michael sighed, as he slumped into the leather chair in the lobby. He watched the last of the employees pass through the revolving door and leaned toward his friend. "I hire, I train, and I wait. Then I motivate, until I reach the point where I have to make demands. Then I wait again. Then I fire. Then I hire again. And always the same result." He shook his head. "It's getting bad, Chad. I've used every ace in my hand trying to get this thing to work. We've got to get our act together soon."

"What are you going to do?" Chad asked.

"I need to find someone who can take over the day-to-day stuff. I get so bogged down in the details that I never get around to what's really important."

"What do you—"

Michael cut his friend off. "I want to plan and establish stronger client relationships. I want to be innovative and creative. I want to lead my team to success." He shook his head. "What they say is true. The work ethic in our country is dead. You can't motivate these people. They don't want to be empowered. They sit around and whine and resist the smallest change. They don't care about objectives. That's it. They just don't care."

Chad jumped in. "I just read a great book on motivation and setting objectives called—"

"Whatever." Michael threw his hands up in surrender. "Look, I've read every book that exists on leadership. And I've been to management training." He stood up and glared at his friend.

"Please. Do me a favor. Don't recommend another book. Give me what I need to get results."

Unlocking and Delivering What Can Be

Over the past decades, society has made remarkable advances that affect how we live and operate. Innovations are getting us out to Mars and deep into the cells of the human body. Manufacturing is becoming more efficient. Vast amounts of information are stored on chips the size of a pinhead. The international business community is expanding every day.

In contrast, progress has been remarkably flat when it comes to improvements in how people function together and how people perform—*how leadership is executed*. Innovations around us are realizing only fractions of their potential as they are trampled by the elephant in the office. The demand to find the key to Leadership Lock is great.

"It is becoming increasingly clear that the demands being placed on today's businesses require a new medic's response," a plant manager with 2,500 employees told us. "The patient has become immune to the old medication."

Innovative leadership is the only phenomenon that will leverage all of society's other innovations. Leadership—of ourselves and others—is what can release us to our full potential. All the changes that would make organizations more profitable, strengthen our education systems, and help our families and communities become more vibrant can be accomplished in only one way—by innovating how leadership happens.

 Having the right employee is a must to be competitive. Being the right leader is a must to win. How effectively are you unlocking what you and others are capable of doing?

What the world needs now is Wellness Culture leadership. What it has is you.

How Important Is Unlocking Leadership?

Why is unlocking leadership important? Because one person operating at a ho-hum level, regardless of position, infects countless others. Employees suffer. The bottom line plummets. Investors get anxious, and families lose their dreams.

Conversely, when people take it upon themselves to break the Leadership Lock—the gap between what is and what could be—they then align people and purpose, and change happens. Progress occurs. Results improve.

For instance, look at Aaron Hilkemann, CEO of Duncan Aviation in Lincoln, Nebraska, and Skip Madsen, former executive vice president and chief operations officer of Duncan

Aviation in Battle Creek, Michigan. Before Aaron and Skip arrived at Battle Creek, the culture was not ideal. Employees were focused on following the rules rather than "doing the right thing." A very rigid organizational structure existed and employees needed to develop trust. Sales and net profits had reached a plateau.

In the first four years under Aaron and Skip's leadership, Battle Creek's sales rose from $35 million to $70 million, and they are still growing. Within two years, the quality ratings in customer surveys moved the company from "off the map" to number two in the industry. In the third year, Duncan landed at number 65 on the list of *Fortune* magazine's top 100 companies to work for, climbing each year to number 25.

How can a company achieve such improvements after years of flat growth? The company had the same employees, the same building and budgets. It served the same industry and used the same marketing and sales vehicles. What changed?

One variable changed: the leadership approach.

Two people and their teams unlocked what was possible. They chose to close the gap between how they operated and what they knew to be effective leadership actions. As a result, people around them began to behave differently. The Wellness Culture grew. When the employees functioned differently, the company's targeted results became a reality.

Aaron and Skip are rare leaders who do not use intellectual rhetoric or emotional pretense to bring about change. Their leadership strategy does not include manipulating people or outcomes. Rather, they consistently deliver results by unlocking their leadership through innovative steps. "True leadership is all about creating effective change. Each time I think I have a problem with an employee or a project, I look at my own areas of Leadership Lock. I go upstream to see what I can do differently," says Skip.

"Invariably, each time I get upstream to
the cause variables, I find no one but myself.
It's how I am responding to a person or what
I am doing with a project that's causing
the results I'm getting."

 What advantages do you give yourself,
your team and your family if you
intentionally take not just proactive
steps but also innovative actions to
break Leadership Lock?

CHAPTER 9

Where Is Your Leadership Lock?

Unlock the Lock and Release Results

All of us encounter challenges or hurdles that impede our ability to obtain the results we envision. Many feel challenged by the need to bring about effective, efficient change. Others would like to create full engagement and motivation in those around them. Other leaders wonder what it takes to run productive meetings. Some want to elicit greater alignment and accountability from those around them. Some desperately want to get more things done. Others seek a better work–life balance. Some of us are simply searching for ways to accomplish things faster and better.

Most leaders have a central issue on their to-do list, an area that, once unlocked, will release the results they know are possible.

There is a time and a place to philosophize and theorize about leadership, but this is not it. This is the time to run the elephant out of the office. We encourage you to put the tools

51

that are introduced in this book into immediate action as you read about them. Begin by choosing an area of Leadership Lock you have encountered. Then, as you move through the leadership technology in the following pages, simply plug it into your area of Leadership Lock.

In working with leaders around the world, we have observed and heard about countless areas of Leadership Lock. The chart that follows is a snapshot of the most common, regardless of type or size of organization or world location.

Leadership Lock	How It Manifests
We need to execute and do what we say we're going to do.	"We are falling behind the pace in our industry."
We need to get faster and better.	"Why is our team so resistant to every new idea?"
Quality. Quality. Quality.	"If they had a choice, would our employees buy our product?"
I've got to do something about my home life.	"Home has become a pit stop on my way back to work."
I need to delegate more effectively, drive cleaner execution.	"It seems like I have to do everything. I haven't used all my vacation days in years."
I simply want to feel good again.	"Aren't we supposed to be enjoying this?"

Leadership Lock	How It Manifests
I'm overwhelmed. I can't get to the things that really need to get done.	"We always seem to be in crisis mode."
We just need to be on the same page.	"True alignment would cut our problems in half."
Balance. I need balance.	"At home we're just running a business called 'Household, Inc.'"
We need to get everyone engaged and on board.	"Things seem to take twice as long as projected; the rework is killing us."
We need our meetings to be more effective.	"Our meetings are torture sessions—one person does all the talking, egos manipulate the agenda, and nothing gets done."

We have studied and worked with thousands of people who have faced the same or similar Leadership Locks you may have identified. These people have successfully moved beyond their areas of Leadership Lock with an innovative approach. In a sense, this book is their story.

You have already seen several items presented with this symbol.

We hope you took the time to answer the questions presented next to the elephant-stomping logos. We encourage you to get even more input and insight by posing the same questions in a larger group.

People around the world are discovering how vital it is to build a powerful Wellness Culture, which indeed is the mother of all strategies. They are creating novel and effective ways to put an end to the toxic workplace, get more done, and become excited about work again. One of these approaches is called *elephant-stomping groups*. These are small groups of three to eight peers who meet regularly to discuss the tools and concepts in this book. When you hold these meetings, this much is guaranteed: Leadership capability will expand and your culture will become more aligned with your strategy objectives. The result? The elephant-stomping groups will build the bottom line.

Feedback from people who have participated in such groups is almost unanimous, albeit said in different ways: "Each and every concept and tool got clearer and sharper as we internalized the material even deeper; teamwork improved and results came faster as we shared tools and solutions specific to our own personal and group issues." Another frequently mentioned benefit: "My home life is much better since I started plugging in 'family' for 'organization' in many of the questions."

If you are interested in applying the concepts and tools in this book to more quickly reach your business and personal objectives, and you think an elephant-stomping group or groups might be effective within your organization, please see the brief and easy-to-follow guidelines for starting your own elephant-stomping group in Appendix A (page 321).

For those who are interested in more details and support, a companion workbook is available free online at www.stomptheelephant.com.

Part Three

DELIVERING ELEPHANT-FREE PRODUCTIVITY

People are not flawed—it is the approach
to the process of change that is flawed.
People do not resist change;
they resist being changed.

What ideas do people believe in?
Almost without exception,
these are their own ideas . . .

CHAPTER 10

A Wellness Culture Tool: The 3 Conditions That Support Change

Honor These Conditions and Get More Done

The world is changing—fast. To stay in business, let alone beat your competition, your results tomorrow will have to be better than they are today. This means one thing: change.

Hundreds of books have been written about change. Countless people have dispensed their wisdom on the subject in seminars, classes, trainings, on the Internet and more. But what if creating change is not as difficult as some people are making it? What if all you needed to know about successful change could be condensed into a formula that fits on the back of a business card?

While change includes many subtle components as well, almost all of the advice essentially reveals three conditions that are invariably part of every effective change initiative. Together they constitute a tool that allows and supports productive change—and it all fits on a business card.

The 3 Conditions
That Support Change

1. **Participants in the change process feel good about themselves.**
2. **The process includes participants' ideas.**
3. **The process includes participants' motivations.**

How can such apparently simple ideas clear up all the conflict and resistance that usually accompany change? Here are the expanded explanations of what these conditions mean and what they look like when implemented.

The 3 Conditions That
Support Change in Action

Rich Crawford said, "You've got to connect culture and strategy. If you don't start there, you'll waste a lot of time." As noted earlier in this book, Rich and his team have led the O-I Latin American Region to outstanding results. Rich continued: "The people who execute the strategies have to understand and own their role in it. That's culture."

But not everyone understands this, which makes Rich laugh. "I have a chart that I use with my team—it shows our vision, mission and strategic objectives. I had a visitor from another organization in my office, and he's incredibly frustrated. He does these surveys—all focused on making things faster and better—and they completely miss that it's the people. So many leaders make it more difficult than it is.

"We know where we need to go—and it begins by getting the people together and creating a culture so they can do it."

How does Rich do it? "My role is to develop leadership and connect my people with the strategic objectives of the organization. What I have to do is build a team and show that team exactly how they fit with those strategies. And we do it with leadership tools that provide a common language. The 3 Conditions That Support Change is one of those tools."

Mark Weir, manufacturing manager for O-I Latin America, explained how Rich and his team used the 3 Conditions That Support Change.

Before their assignment in Latin America, Rich and Mark were asked to go to Europe in 2003. Owens-Illinois, the world's largest glass producer, had just purchased BSN, and named the expanded organization O-I. To date, BSN was the company's largest acquisition. Rich and his team were put in charge of leading the integration.

Integrations after acquisitions are often referred to as battlegrounds. Plus, this one was not as simple as walking down the hallway into another office. Rich and his team had to make it happen on both sides of the Atlantic. Not an easy chore.

Rich went to work immediately by honoring the first condition—*participants feel good about themselves*—with his team.

Mark said, "Rich would call us two to three times a day. He would check on us. Not to see if we were getting our work done but to ask how we were doing personally. He wanted to see if we had our needs met and to see how he could help.

"Our mission was to do whatever we could do to make the acquisition a success. We knew that started with bringing people together. The key was creating face time at all the plants. So, at every plant across Europe, we'd start off with a presentation. 'We are one O-I,' we told them. And, 'We are going to get aligned as one operating body.'"

Anyone who is in business is apt to have an upset stomach as he reads those remarks. Sadly, the business world is famous for poorly executed acquisitions—and many of those efforts start with well-intentioned rhetoric much like Mark's words above.

What differentiates O-I's efforts, though, is that Mark and Rich *continued* by ensuring they honored the 3 Conditions That Support Change. Here is how.

Mark said, "In each presentation, we quickly asked questions. Then we continued with questions throughout our time together. Everyone would share their answers verbally, and other times they would write down answers on sticky notes, so everyone had a voice. This got people engaged and motivated toward where we all wanted to go."

Here are some of the questions Mark and the team asked:

- What can you do to personally ensure that we have the most successful integration possible?

- What do you think is the most significant priority we can focus on to ensure this process is a success?

- Why do you want to see this integration go smoothly?

- What can we do more of that will help you become more successful?

"The beauty of this is that we got people engaged," said Mark. "We got feedback we wouldn't have gotten, which allowed us to adapt. We used the questions so we could discover their ideas and motivations.

"For instance, one guy answered the last question with 'I'd like to see more operations. In the past we weren't allowed to do that.'

"So we took that idea to new levels. We took five plant managers to the United States, showed them three or four operations, and gave them a tour of O-I headquarters. Then Rich asked our then-CEO, Steve McCracken, to spend five minutes with them. Steve said, 'No—I want more time with them. I want them to know how important they are!'"

The 3 Conditions That Support Change gave the O-I team a formula to follow—and it delivered for them.

Mark said: "We have now seen improvements in *all* key metrics. Our original goal was to create synergies savings in the amount of well over one hundred million Euros, and achieve this in three years. It has been less than two years since we started, and we are ninety-nine percent there."

There was an additional result that was not an original objective.

"This may seem small, but it says a lot," said Mark. "When I went back to visit one of the plants, they were quite proud to show me their Christmas tree. There, right behind the tree, they had taken down the BSN sign and replaced it with an O-I banner, and they put up a U.S. flag right next to their German flag. This was the best Christmas present I ever received. What this symbolized is that *they* had made the transition."

Unfortunately, across all industries, most leaders report that it is not a common practice to honor the 3 Conditions That Support Change—ensuring that people feel good about themselves, seeking and using others' ideas, and tapping into motivations.

Rich summed it up: "There are plenty of leaders who say, 'I don't know about all this soft stuff.' Well, this soft stuff is really the job of the leader.

"If the leader doesn't get people together,
build the culture, and generate synergy,
people will revert to the old habits of turf
protection and defensiveness. Then,
the only thing that changes is the
name over the door."

CHAPTER 11

Leaders Who Make Change Harder Than It Has to Be

You Can Make Change Easier

The most successful businesses are generally those whose products and services evolve along with—or even ahead of—customer needs. To what extent does the success of your organization rely on change? What percentage of your work life is devoted to promoting healthy change? Many of the leaders we work with report that 90 percent of their work is about leading effective change.

How effective are you when you:

- Want someone to stop or start doing something?

- Need to improve your skill set or someone else's?

- Need to create a more effective working relationship with your boss?

- Want to create greater opportunities for yourself or others?

- Need to enhance personal or business results?

- Need to get better at delegating work?

- Have to develop a more effective procedure or system?

- Want to build stronger relationships with customers?

- Have to get better at cultivating ideas and shepherding them to fruition?

- Want to increase sales or lower expenses?

Leaders like Rich and Mark, above, are masterful at creating change—for themselves, their organizations and the people they lead.

Although they work with the same or similar circumstances as their peers in other organizations—deadlines, budgets, staffing issues, profit-and-loss pressures—because they honor the 3 Conditions That Support Change, they are able to achieve superior results.

What differences would show up in your career, your personal life and the lives of those around you if you strengthened your ability to facilitate healthy change in the leadership moments that pepper a day?

Make Change Hard or Make It Easy

A discouraging fact: The idea of change instills fear, discomfort and confusion in many organizations. When asked, most leaders report that the majority of their change efforts take more time than projected, devour more resources than allocated, and in many cases do not accomplish strategies. When this happens, you know there is Leadership Lock; an elephant is on the rampage.

In some cases, leaders say their attempts to create change actually backfire; the elephant sits at the door chomping on their return on investment; the culture takes a significant hit; and resistance festers in the workforce. When such Leadership Lock cripples a team, people lose their excitement, relationships suffer, rapport and trust implode, creativity is squelched, and the revolving door of leadership begins to spin.

What if some of the precepts some leaders have learned regarding how to facilitate change are wrong? What if we have been making change harder than it needs to be? Imagine the difference it would make if healthy change were a natural function, owned and driven by every member of your team.

A Case Study in Futility: Cindy's Change Conundrum

"Cindy, I've known you for many years," her CEO said. "I would never have pushed the board to hire you as president if I hadn't thought you had what it took to get the job done." He stepped out of the door, then looked back her. "But I have to tell you, we're in deep water. Something better change." The door clicked shut behind him.

"Change," muttered Cindy. She slumped into the leather chair behind her desk. "That's all I've been trying to do here is get people to change." She stared at the ceiling. "And now I'm starting to talk to myself."

The ceiling had no answers. She looked at the bookcase to her left, her eyes randomly surfing the titles on each shelf. Nearly a third of those leadership and business books addressed change. She knew because she had read every one of them. "Yet we're still stuck," she thought. "What is it I'm missing? What is it I haven't done?"

She went over her checklist:

1. *"I've got the right people on the team."* In her first two years, she had replaced six of her nine VPs. "They're a talented bunch. That's not the problem."

2. *"I've got the resources."* If anything, this was her area of expertise. She and the CEO were considered financial wizards on the street.

3. *"The infrastructure is sound."* Yes, the firm was heavily matrixed, but everyone had a clear understanding of their roles.

4. *"We have a clear objective."* Everyone has been told what he or she has to do.

5. *"We've proved in the past that we can dominate the market."* Facts were facts. Her company had held a dominant position, but that advantage had eroded.

Cindy clenched her teeth. Every time she and her top team analyzed this monster or brought in a consultant, they came up with the same list of problems:

- The company is stuck in a box and is not innovative.

- Production costs are too high.

- Execution is shoddy and inefficient.

In short, they had to get better and faster—and soon. She, her team and their consultants had identified the obstacles. They had set goals for each business unit, carefully crafted implementation plans, and communicated them to the entire organization. Yet they had little to show for their efforts.

In fact, not only was pressure from the board mounting but pulse surveys showed that the employees—the people she wanted to lead to greatness—were beginning to grumble.

Cindy closed her eyes. What was holding them back? Her breathing tightened and her neck tensed as she realized she might not have the answers.

CHAPTER 12

The Traditional Approach to Change: A Formula for Staying Stuck

The Common Approach Commonly Fails

In the preceding case study, Cindy applied everything she had learned in an effort to bring about change, which is exactly what had gotten her into the mess she was in. She used an old, standard formula for change that created resistance among employees and diminished her organization's return on investment.

The traditional approach to change consists of four steps:

Step 1: Identify the problem.
Step 2: Have an "expert" determine a solution.
Step 3: Tell people how to change.
Step 4: Try to overcome the resistance created by the first three steps.

Cindy satisfied step 1: *Identify the problem.* This did not take long. Problems were the topic of most meetings she attended.

Cindy satisfied step 2: *Have an expert determine a solution.* She and her top team had held numerous strategy meetings. Along with leading industry consultants, they had devised airtight plans for leading the company out of its conundrum. It was their job to do so, Cindy reasoned. After all, they were hired to lead the company.

Cindy satisfied step 3: *Tell people how to change.* She and her team delivered the plans to their immediate reports, who then cascaded the strategies to the rest of the employees.

Cindy is now left with the task of satisfying step 4: *Try to overcome the resistance created by the first three steps.* This is the point at which she begins looking at the ceiling for answers. Her confusion provides convincing evidence that she is unaware of who or what is causing the resistance and poor results.

The Costs of the Traditional Approach to Change

The traditional approach to change has numerous variations. Without effective leadership, the basic procedure is the same—and so are the results:

- It takes a long time to get things done.

- Revenue is lost.

- Future initiatives for change are sabotaged.

- Morale suffers.

- Careers are prematurely terminated.

- Work relationships and job satisfaction deteriorate.

- People tiptoe around the elephant in the office.

Accomplished leaders are replacing the traditional approach to change with a new formula based on a different paradigm.

They realize that how people handle change determines whether the organization moves backward or forward. For them, change does not portend danger; it signals opportunity.

CHAPTER 13

If Change Is Constant, Why Won't My Team Change?

How Bosses Slow Their Teams Down

It is ironic: Change is difficult for many people and organizations, yet change is a law of the universe. Like gravity, change is inevitable; nature mandates it. Evolution is continuous. Individuals and companies that do not change eventually find themselves out of the race.

Could it be that *not* getting in the way of change is an ingredient of effective leadership?

You Are Wrong and Need Fixing

Steven Vannoy: "For years I subscribed to the adage that you can't teach an old dog new tricks. Unwittingly, I falsely capped my own potential and that of others by believing that some people are flawed, that some people do not change. Yet this idea directly conflicted with another truth I embrace: Change is constant.

> **"This could mean only one thing: People are not flawed—it is the approach to the process of change that is flawed. People do not resist change; they resist being changed.**

"Years ago, before I grasped this wisdom, my marriage was in jeopardy. My wife and I desperately wanted our union to work. We wanted to change. So we went to a marriage counselor. What we didn't know was that this person was terribly misguided; he focused primarily on the problems in our relationship. Looking back, I can see that the result was predictable. As he focused on our problems and told us what we had to do to change, we became more defensive, the problems grew worse, the chasm widened, and we divorced.

"What would have happened if the therapist's approach to change had been different? What if, through questions, he had directed us to focus on what was working in our relationship? What would have happened if we had discussed what we wanted more of rather than what we wanted the other person to stop doing? How would we have grown had we acknowledged each other for the qualities we brought to the relationship rather than the qualities we lacked?"

Enlightened people realize how backward it is to think someone is wrong. Like blazing neon signs, those who tell others how they need to change communicate destructive messages to those at the receiving end:

- You and what you are doing are wrong; therefore, you need fixing.

- You are not capable of contributing in a valuable way.

- Your ideas do not count.

Effective leaders understand that others would not have said what they said or done what they did if they did not think they were right. When a leader communicates that another person is wrong, the person usually builds a psychological wall that limits communication, impedes synergy, destroys teams, and slows change. Elephants thrive in cultures where walls and silos exist.

Ineffective attempts to facilitate change usually yield similar results. The following questions can reveal if Leadership Lock exists in the area of leading change:

- Are changes taking too long?

- Are the processes used to facilitate change more frustrating than you think they need to be?

- Are the organization's efforts consuming more resources than necessary?

- Are results falling short of expectations?

- Are your team's efforts to bring about change causing resistance and hurting professional relationships?

- Are past failures setting up future initiatives to fail even before they are launched?

- Is the effort to create change eroding people's confidence in their leaders?

Here is a leader who is discovering how to handle change successfully. "Our plant manager asked me to address the volume production peaks that were affecting our department overtime and forcing us to continuously change our production schedules," Gonzalo Cienfuegos of the Procter & Gamble plant in Naucalpan, Mexico, said. "I tried meeting several times with the three production planners to convince them we had a problem and have them start working on it. This didn't work.

"Then I spoke to the most experienced planner and made her accountable to coordinate a proposal from the three to get the objective done. That didn't work either.

"Eventually, I realized their reluctance to move forward was due to their convictions about flexibility, and that was why nothing was working. So I organized a meeting of employees from logistics and operations to address my plant manager's expectations.

"In that meeting, as soon as I began telling these people what we had to do, they started saying it would never work, it couldn't be done. I was about to yell at them that this was our plant manager's expectation and they had to do it whether they liked it or not."

But Gonzalo did not yell—and the elephant stayed out of the office. He resisted the temptation to use the traditional approach to change. "I realized at that moment I was trying to control them," he said. "I was trying to fix their way of thinking."

Instead, Gonzalo did something else; he used the 3 Conditions That Support Change.

1. To ensure that the team began to *feel better about themselves*, he acknowledged them in a sincere, specific and selective way for the contributions and efforts they had been making.

2. He *included their ideas* by seeking their perspectives and opinions. "Simply listening to them made a difference. And there were ideas we hadn't considered," Gonzalo noted.

3. He *identified their motivations* by asking them why it was important to them that they deliver results of high quality.

Gonzalo was rewarded for breaking from the standard. He said, "This new approach has saved us from wasting a lot of work hours in fruitless meetings. We'll have a lot more control during the high season."

Leading by Facilitating
Instead of Controlling

The new formula for facilitating change is not about being weak or condoning poor results. It is not about settling for less than what is needed.

It is about accomplishing more than we envision. It is about building partnerships so we can move forward with greater fluidity. It is about guiding and facilitating rather than limiting through control.

Facilitating change means incorporating different opinions and motivations. Understanding that differences of opinion constitute an organization's strength is imperative. This approach means realizing there is something that makes each person tick and discovering what that is.

It All Depends on You

Some people do not want to face the fact that if a person is not effective, if his career is stalled and results are poor, it is usually because of one primary factor: This person cannot bring about appropriate changes.

An NCAA Division I college basketball coach was interviewed by the media after his team played their best game of the season. Asked what he told his team after the game, he said, "I told them how disappointing it was that it took this long for them to learn to play hard for an entire game."

The coach's career ended shortly after this. Why? Two reasons: He had not been able to bring about change—his team had not learned to play hard for an entire game—and he blamed the team members for their inability to learn this lesson. In reality, whose responsibility was it to effectively teach the team this lesson?

People who keep the elephant out of the office propel themselves to higher levels because of their accountability to themselves. If things are not moving forward fast enough, these people examine their own behavior first. Then they apply a leadership tool to create different results.

John Slieter, vice president of sales at Duncan Aviation in Lincoln, Nebraska, is an enlightened leader. He said, "The 3 Conditions That Support Change is an important checklist that I have intuitively known for some time but never completely honored. In addition to immediately creating greater results for my team, this tool cleared my head of all the cumbersome leadership strategies I had accumulated over the years. It altered the game."

CHAPTER 14

Change Condition #1: Participants in the Change Process Feel Good about Themselves

This Change Condition Is an Elephant Killer

People who do not feel good about themselves are unlikely to change because:

- Change means they have been doing something wrong.

- Change requires more effort or a different effort.

- Change can make people feel insecure, at risk of exposing a perceived weakness or revealing they do not have the answers.

- Change can require giving up perceived power.

Even with the best-laid plans, even when lucrative incentives are offered, the wise leader knows that people who do not feel good about themselves are likely to deliver marginal results at best in any change initiative.

People who do not feel good about themselves often have common responses to initiatives for change. These responses are often the elephants in the office. Do you recognize any of these responses?

- *Victim mentality:* "I can't get my job done because I never get the resources I need. And watch: When this initiative bombs, I'll be the one who gets blamed."

- *Defeatist mentality:* "It'll never work because it's a stupid idea in the first place."

- *Insecurity:* "It wasn't my idea—and I'll make sure they understand why they should have used my idea instead!"

- *Apathy:* "Why should I care about this?"

- *Fear of full participation:* "What happens if we don't succeed?"

- *Withdrawal:* "If I don't talk or contribute, maybe this whole thing will go away."

- *Passivity:* "I've seen this approach before; this too shall pass if I just wait it out."

- *Focus on why it won't work:* "We don't have enough ____ (fill in the blank)."

- *Fatigue:* "I just don't have the energy for this that I used to."

- *Spreading negative attitudes like a cancer:* "Hey, did you hear about the crazy ideas they've cooked up now?"

How seriously do you take your responsibility to foster the development of capable, resilient, inspired and engaged people around you? The least effective organizations operate with the notion that society has a responsibility to provide them with an outstanding talent pool. They hire new recruits, give them a fair paycheck and expect them to deliver accordingly. But in a short time they find themselves lamenting that the new hire did not have the character or skill they thought he had. Like ringleaders at a circus, they shout and direct, shuffle the person around, hire someone new, and begin the process all over again.

Successful organizations avoid the high costs of employee attrition because they realize their company is just as responsible as the rest of society for helping others realize their potential.

These organizations build cultures that cultivate confident, productive workers. This approach helps people feel good about themselves *in advance of, during* and *after* the natural, ongoing cycles of change in business. Consequently, these employees are not threatened by change. They see change as an opportunity to move forward.

You will see the approach people in such organizations use, but first, what is the opposite strategy?

We Are Not Talking about Pizza Parties

Unskilled leaders (often referred to as bosses) may rely on a bag of tricks to help employees feel good about themselves. Sadly, these people unwittingly create toxic cultures within their organizations and suppress results.

Consider the following strategies from the bag of "feel good" tricks and the results they usually produce:

1. *Strategy*: The Pizza Party Ploy. *Result*: In an unhealthy work culture, this type of strategy can make employees feel manipulated rather than truly appreciated and can serve to cement cliques and promote the circulation of destructive rumors. Office elephants become fat by eating a lot of pizzas.

2. *Strategy*: The "Just Trust Me" Tactic. *Result*: By feeling the need to make such a request—"Just trust me on this"—the person has provided another reason to be considered untrustworthy. A leader who does not share the thinking behind decisions sends the message that input from employees or family members is not wanted and that they are not expected to fully participate.

3. *Strategy*: The Bonus Boomerang. *Result*: In an unhealthy culture, bonuses often promote the perception that "we're doing this for the money." Although bonuses can be effective, a reward system driven solely by bonuses has long-term destructive results because there will never be enough bonuses. In addition, bonuses create unequal classes of people because typically the same people earn them repeatedly. In these situations, bonuses potentially turn off more people than they encourage. Finally, the bonus-only approach diminishes the possibility that people will focus on the higher purpose for doing what they do—their internal motivation.

4. *Strategy*: Conniving Compliments. *Result*: Compliments that are insincere, nonspecific and too frequent may manipulate others in the short term but do little to build self-esteem and trusting relationships.

A culture in which employee self-esteem depends on external motivators like those from this bag of tricks cannot move forward. There are not enough tricks to sustain such a culture in the long term. Successful leaders realize this, so they rely on more effective, simpler and more affordable strategies to ensure that participants in the change process feel good about themselves.

What is the opposite of pizza parties? Here are some Wellness Culture strategies that honor the 3 Conditions That Support Change:

- *Building a culture that allows people to excel, to be their best.* Members of such a culture own their work and know they are contributing to something that matters. They come to work not because they have to but because they choose to.

- *Fostering full, free, two-way information flow.* When participants can process information, meaning they were not communicated *at* but participated *in* open exchange of information, there are fewer gaps in information that they need to speculate about. When gaps exist, they are often filled with misconceptions and inaccurate information (read: rumors).

- *Articulating clear, achievable and challenging objectives that can be fully understood and supported by all parties.* Participants who understand what is important—and why—do not need micromanaging.

- *Co-creating a plan of execution that is owned by all parties.* Determining how to achieve an objective is just as important as identifying the objective.

- *Tapping into people's motivations.* When people believe in an idea and can envision its benefits to themselves and their goals, they own it.

- *Acknowledging people's contributions.* Unlike conniving compliments from a bag of tricks, acknowledgments that are sincere, specific and selective provide usable feedback and reinforce outstanding behavior and results.

What percentage of people honor this first condition that supports change—that participants in the change process feel good about themselves? We have asked thousands of people this question, and the response almost always falls in the range of 10 to 25 percent.

**What competitive advantages will you provide
your company—and yourself—by honoring this
first condition that supports change?**

The elephant in the office begins looking for another home
when people feel good about themselves.

Are Your Compliments Hurting Others?

With the best of intentions, some people give a lot of compliments. But their words do little good, and in many cases, they
hurt relationships, create rebellion and destroy future results.

Why? Too often, compliments are not completely **sincere**;
they are a sly attempt to get others to do it our way. Also, they
are rarely **specific**. A general, rah-rah statement like "Hey,
good job today" is nearly useless. Finally, compliments are not
selective; they may come too frequently or not often enough.
In these cases, they lose their significance and are quickly
tuned out.

If you use the tool called the 3 S's of Yes—sincere, specific
and selective—your acknowledgments can enhance people's
perspectives of themselves and the tasks at hand. When used
effectively, the 3 S's create a new focus. This directly impacts
behaviors and results.

A Wellness Culture Tool: The 3 S's of Yes

Sincere. With sincerity, acknowledgments are authentic
and free of hidden objectives. *Julie, the work you did on this
project has taken our team far beyond what we ever envi-
sioned. Thank you for your commitment to our common goal.*

Specific. Specificity ensures that the receivers know exactly
which action or attitude they have delivered that is making a

difference. *Julie, your willingness to learn that new computer program is allowing us to move faster in the execution of our strategy.* As a result, Julie has an enhanced perspective of who she is and what she can do. You can be sure she will continue to cultivate and enhance her willingness to learn.

Selective. Compliments need to be given selectively, with proper frequency. For example, a child—or adult, for that matter—who hears "good job!" ten times a day will quickly tune you out. Additionally, people who never receive acknowledgments will also join the disengaged.

Want to give a compliment? Find the opportunity to add value, to serve the recipient's life and development, and go for it.

CHAPTER 15

Change Condition #2: The Process Includes Participants' Ideas

Forget "Buy-in"— Develop "Ownership" Instead

Some people create significant changes within their organizations because they understand a simple truth: People will work diligently to implement ideas they believe in.

What ideas do people believe in? Almost without exception, these are their own ideas or those they created with others.

Too often, the "ivory tower" approach is used: Some leader somewhere determines a solution. This person then has to use his waking hours selling his idea to others in the hope that those executing the plan will buy in.

Achieving buy-in ensures that organizational results will lag; people would rather not buy something they can develop and own themselves.

The packaging manager at a plant in Cleveland, Tennessee, used the second condition for change as a key to addressing his area of Leadership Lock. The general manager told us the results:

"For a long time we had tried to find a way to save on the expense of the products we specially prepare for our largest customer.

"Because of their special packaging requirements, we've had to slow down the line to sixty to seventy-five percent of efficiency. To solve this puzzle, our packaging manager used the 3 Conditions That Support Change with his team. During the process of asking the team various questions, a mechanic proposed a solution that simply required switching the order of the assembly process. This idea alone will save us $200,000 a year. Better yet, because the team came up with the idea, they ran with its implementation. Not bad for the application of one leadership tool."

 When was the last time you resisted one of your own great ideas? Conversely, what percentage of the time do you get excited and charge forward with other people's ideas?

Employees whose ideas are not solicited, heard or used generally exhibit predictable and conspicuous responses, including:

- *Lack of motivation.* "I don't know how to do this because I haven't been told."

- *Disengagement.* "It doesn't matter if this gets done or not. They'll come up with another idea to save us."

- *Reluctance to contribute.* "We shouldn't be doing it this way, but I'm keeping my mouth shut."

- *Limited investment in results.* "Just do what you have to. It's almost Friday."

- *Sabotage.* "This is stupid. I'm going to make sure they bomb on this one."

What happens within a team when we ask other people for their ideas rather than imposing our own? "When it comes to problem solving, planning and improving processes, I'm continually amazed at the difference between one person's ideas versus the ideas of two or three or four people," noted the president of a service company who has adopted this tool.

The 3 Conditions That Support Change align people with purpose before implementation begins. Graham Orriss, operations manager at the Procter & Gamble plant in Oxnard, California, said it this way: "You're going to get everyone's input at some point—either during the effort or after it's completed. You choose."

"We have become quite intimate with the 3 Conditions That Support Change, so much so that now, if we fail to honor them, it really sticks out," said a mid-level manager at a consumer health organization. "Just a few weeks ago, we unveiled an adaptation to an inventory system. One of the employees remarked that what we were doing to them felt like a forced march.

"This was our wake-up call. The person was right, and we quickly adapted by asking for the team's ideas on how to improve the plan we had offered." The manager smiled. "Of course—no surprise to any of us—the ideas they came up with exceeded what we had originally planned. Plus, now we have peace of mind that the new system will be carried out. And that's priceless."

How priceless? A plant in the Gerber Baby Food system needed to improve efficiencies in the production of their glass containers. By using the 3 Conditions That Support Change, they created elephant-free productivity; ideas generated by line employees dropped glass breakage by over 50 percent.

We often ask people how many leaders honor this second condition of the 3 Conditions That Support Change. Their responses consistently land between 5 and 10 percent.

How will gathering and implementing more of your team members' ideas take any brakes off change initiatives you face? How will honoring this condition enhance your own effectiveness and affect your career?

Soliciting Others' Ideas

Some effective strategies for soliciting and harvesting employees' ideas include:

- Up front, articulate what is important to achieve and why. Create the context from which future questions will be asked.

- Ask questions that address objectives, execution, motivations and accountability. Average leaders are crying for help in developing these four areas within their teams. Leaders whose teams are excelling go right to the source for their solutions: They ask their teams. For example:

1. *Objective:* "Where do you want to be with this project by the end of the week?" And, "What was your criterion for setting this mark?"

2. *Execution:* "What will be your priority action steps to achieve your objective?" And, "What resource planning do you want to do in advance?"

3. *Motivation:* "As you consider delivering the finished product, what most excites you?" And, "What are the most important ramifications for the organization when you deliver this project on time?"

4. *Accountability:* "As you move through the week, how will you assess if you are making adequate progress?" And, "As you execute your strategy, what are your standards for quality?"

- When possible, allow employee ideas to stand. Taking employee suggestions seriously in a brainstorming session encourages creativity and fosters a culture of engagement. Asking for someone else's ideas and then adding your own brilliant idea on top of theirs guarantees the other person will soon shut down. The exception: when a group of individuals agree to build on each other's ideas for the sake of sculpting a powerful solution.

- Implement employee ideas whenever possible. Demonstrate the value of employee ideas by putting them into action. Giving employees this kind of reinforcement will increase their ownership in the effort and improve results.

- Give credit where credit is due. By using the 3 S's of Yes, as described earlier, leaders assure employees of the value of their contributions—which means they will contribute more. "Because of your idea, we reduced glass breakage, which helped us to reach our quarterly profit-and-loss goal."

Can You Include the Ideas
of 13,000 People?

In his first year as president of a division within a Fortune 500 company, one leader led his team through dramatic changes in a very short time, improving the bottom line by more than $200 million. With 13,000 employees, he obviously could not ask for everyone's ideas. Did this mean that honoring the 3 Conditions That Support Change was not an option for him?

Not only is the answer no but, in this situation, honoring these three conditions was critical. He had to change the way work was getting done. He knew that if he used the older, traditional approach of trying to control all the steps involved in the initiative for change, he would fail miserably. Instead, he took four important steps:

- *He provided training for his leadership team.* One of this leader's first steps in his new position was to train his leadership team in the 3 Conditions That Support Change. He knew that getting where they needed to go would require more than any single person could provide.

- *He collected data, ideas and suggestions and then set clear objectives.* Ideally, he would have co-created all of the division's objectives with his colleagues. But timing required his direction at an early stage. After collecting the necessary information, he was able to set the course for his team by establishing the primary objectives.

- *He empowered his team to co-create the plan for achieving those objectives.* When it came to creating a plan of execution, the president did not waste time getting in his team's way with distracting messages and demands; instead, he tapped into the genius of his team by asking the right questions.

- *He focused on the third of the 3 Conditions That Support Change.* By tapping into the motivations of his leadership team, he inspired them to lead *their* teams in a way that honored the 3 Conditions That Support Change.

At times, not all ideas can be identified, heard or used; yet the participants are unfazed because whatever idea is adopted is a step toward the common objective—a common motivation for many. As this leader reports, "With this tool, you can move mountains."

What Happens If People Still Do Not Change?

The 3 Conditions That Support Change constitute a powerful tool for encouraging new behaviors. But what happens if, even with consistent and appropriate use of this tool, behaviors do not change?

We all know that not everyone grows at the same rate. Not everyone is in the right position, at the right company, or in the professional field that is best suited for him. Timing and circumstances are important, and effective leaders discern this.

Fact: People will change according to their own schedules. Their time lines accelerate when effective leadership technology like the 3 Conditions That Support Change is used. In the end, while there is solid evidence that everyone can change, it is not the leader's job to wait for people to do so. If a leader has used proven tools for change and the employee still has not adapted, successful business leaders know that the person should be retrained, relocated or released.

CHAPTER 16

Change Condition #3: The Process Includes Participants' Motivations

People Who Include Participants' Motivations No Longer Work 24/7

When we prepare to work with new clients, we often ask what their greatest needs are. Overwhelmingly, the request we hear the most is: "I want to learn how to motivate my team. I know they can deliver so much more."

By now you can easily see the paradox in this request. Attempting to motivate others, trying to boost their morale and coax them into being more engaged, is a never-ending task and a severe drain on precious resources, including a leader's time and energy. No matter how effective a leader is at awarding the next perk, providing the next rah-rah speech—or slamming employees with repercussions—these short-term strategies quickly become a drain.

Tapping into another person's *own* motivations is more effective. As a line manager at a western U.S. manufacturing plant observed, "As I've used this tool, one of my biggest ah-ha's is the realization that not everyone is motivated by the same thing I am. This sounds obvious, but I now realize that before this insight, I was trying to falsely motivate others around me. What I was really doing was turning them off."

Using this condition of change has an additional benefit. By discovering the motivations of the people around us, we are better able to understand their behaviors. As a result, we make better decisions that serve them and the organization.

This strategy is not a secret. Yet the leaders who have tapped into their employees' motivations have created an advantage unlike anything that can be bought or sold.

One person creating elephant-free productivity stated it this way:

> **"When I include participants' ideas, I tap into their heads and get brilliant perspectives and suggestions. But when I tap into their motivations, I get something that takes us all to a whole new level: I get their hearts.**

"Now, when my team is completing a project or task, they're doing it for their own reasons instead of doing it for mine. In this situation, change comes rapidly and the team is absolutely unstoppable."

Chucking the Checklist Mentality

Checklists are always a helpful organizational tool. But what happens when employees move through their day with the sole purpose of checking off items on a to-do list given to them by someone else? The result is uninspired people who should not be blamed for being so.

Conversely, when the people around you *own* the items on their lists, they produce high-quality work, take pride in their efforts and communicate effectively.

How much would you be willing to pay for employees who approach each task with their hearts as well as their minds? People who honor the third of the 3 Conditions That Support Change know you do not have to pay such employees extraordinary amounts of money. Though money is an effective and necessary reward, it does not guarantee motivation. Ample research proves this. Motivation is determined by and unique to each employee. People who are effective at tapping into that unique motivation find that their job of influencing results becomes easier.

If we have not successfully used this condition, the behavior of others will give us valuable feedback. Some examples include:

- *I'm doing this just for the paycheck.* Money motivates. But when someone can be heard uttering "Another day, another dollar," there is leadership work to do.

- *I'm doing this to keep my job.* Fear motivates. But everyone who achieves long-term success knows that people motivated by fear do only the minimum required to keep their jobs. Adrenaline soon subsides, and disengagement, sabotage and high turnover rates follow.

- *I'm doing this because I was told to.* This tactic can work in a pinch, but in time people push back; no one appreciates being programmed like a machine.

- *I'm doing this to impress the boss.* This approach guarantees you will get nothing but the boss's ideas in duplicate form, and end up with 1×1, instead of 1×2. The power of two people bringing their talents and perspectives to the same issue always beats one.

- *I'm doing this because I don't want to be yelled at or embarrassed.* This approach guarantees a minimalist effort and is the active ingredient in resentment.

Strategies that support these attitudes are low on the motivational food chain. If relied on heavily, they provide an equally low return on an organization's investment in its staff.

Motivations for Moving Forward

Elephants cannot survive when people are excited, on a roll, and performing at peak levels. When people are in such states, their lists of motivations look like the following:

- *I want to be a part of an outstanding team.* People want to know they belong to a winning team, a team that is engaged and working toward a common, worthwhile goal.

- *I want to make a difference.* One of the strongest human desires is to know we are contributing productively and positively.

- *I want to build my career.* This goal is a strong motivator when the person seeks to build a career through making a difference rather than through indifference to the people around him.

- *I want to be able to live with myself.* At the end of the day, peace of mind in knowing we have done our best is the softest pillow.

- *I want to provide for my family.* For many, this is the ultimate motivation.

- *I want to enjoy the journey.* People who live lives of high quality understand there is no finish line. The work found in each day is the objective.

- *I want to maximize my potential.* For some people, the urge to discover what they can create and achieve during their lives is nearly unquenchable.

- *I want to contribute to the well-being of my teammates.* Genuinely caring for and working to ensure the success of those around us makes us rock-solid pillars of the team.

Motivations like these are a rewarding reminder of the Humanity Factor's impact. They are so powerful in their ability to move people forward that they have residual benefits. Even in teams of two, let alone teams of thousands, it is impossible to always satisfy the second condition that supports change—to include everyone's ideas on every subject—yet the leaders who honor this third condition need not worry. People who have tapped motivations like those above develop strong characters and remain motivated and fully engaged even when the idea being implemented is not their own. They embrace and use the Humanity Factor by staying connected to their dream, their purpose and their internal motivations.

When participants' ideas and motivations are involved, change becomes a natural occurrence, leaving people to wonder: Why would we do it any other way?

How many business leaders consistently honor this third condition that supports change—the process that involves participants' motivations? Our research says 1 to 5 percent.

 What motivates you? What inspires you to operate and interact with others in extraordinary ways?

Leaders Who Invite the Elephant into the Office: The Soapbox or Telling Approach

Perhaps you have had the opportunity to observe leaders around the world. If so, you know that only a few understand that *telling* people what their motivations are is not the same as *discovering* and *honoring* other people's motivations. Many leaders approach this third condition that supports change by *telling* people why something should be important to them.

This soapbox approach of forcing motivations on others levies a heavy tax on the leader's time and on everyone's morale. It ultimately tears down the very thing the leader is attempting to build and drives skeptical employees away from the change initiative.

These people make statements such as:

- "Guys, this project is extremely important to your careers."

- "You've got to reach these goals so you can get your bonuses!"

- "If quality improves, we'll look good to senior management."

- "It's not going to look good on your record if you don't deliver."

- "It's important that you get good grades so you can go to college."

These pleas and pep talks commonly meet with glazed eyes and limited engagement. By approaching their teammates or families or students in such a way, these leaders or parents or teachers reinforce the lowest levels of motivation.

So if telling people does not work, what does?

How to Tap into the Motivations of Others

During a leadership training session, a participant asked, "How do you tap into participants' motivations?" The facilitator stood silently, allowing the rest of the group to consider the question. After a few moments, a voice broke the silence. It came from the corner, from the only person who had no direct reports. Though her voice was soft, those in the room heard her with piercing clarity.

"You ask them," she said.

Questions that can help a leader tap into the motivations of others include:

- What are your reasons for wanting to ensure greater quality?

- What are the reasons why completing this project is important to you?

- How do you think your responsibilities related to this project will contribute to overall results?

- Jill, your enthusiasm is contagious. What is the reason you are so excited about this project?

- Stan, you've been with us for thirty-two years and are here every day, giving your best. What are some of the reasons you've been so loyal to this company?

- What difference do you think using that idea will make?

- What are the reasons it's important to you to be a part of a great team?

- What are your reasons for wanting to achieve these goals?

Leaders who ask questions like these know that the circumstances, the timing and the words they choose will differ with the situation. But they also know that some things remain constant: No matter how hard you try to tell people why they should be motivated, it does not work; everyone has different motivations, and you tap into their motivations by asking effective questions.

When personal motivations are tapped, people take greater ownership, change occurs efficiently, and results improve.

The Quest for the Right Questions

Effective leaders always consider certain elements when asking questions. These elements are addressed in part seven; but three key elements must be discussed here so that the 3 Conditions That Support Change can be applied immediately to your Leadership Lock.

Ask questions you do not already have answers for and for which you are truly open to hearing answers. Demonstrating your sincere interest in other people's experiences and opinions encourages them to be more forthcoming.

Ask questions that are open ended, that cannot be answered by a yes or no. Open-ended questions help courageous people encourage their colleagues to think.

Ask questions that are forward focused. Questions with a forward focus guide the person's energy toward solutions rather than problems, toward what is working rather than what is not working, toward learning lessons rather than finding fault or laying blame.

Imagine your area of Leadership Lock is achieving more effective execution. Here are some sample questions that fit the above criteria and address the Leadership Lock.

- "What are our first and second objectives in delivering this project?" (Instead of this common approach: "Here's what we need to do. What do you think?")

- "What action steps should we make a priority on our calendars to achieve our objectives?" (Rather than this traditional and vague method: "How can I help you?" And, "Do you have any questions?")

- "Given this plan, what other items on our calendar might need to shift?" And "What follow-up actions should we take if there is shifting?" (This contrasts with the traditional backward-focus question that is asked: "Why can't we get more resources to help us?")

- "What benchmarks should we use so we know we're on target?" (Instead of the often asked: "Can I see this when you're done?")

- "How does this fit with our master plan in this area?" (Instead of what typically happens in this regard: No question is asked as everyone assumes—incorrectly—that everyone else understands why the strategy is important.)

Eduardo Cervantes, a section head at Procter & Gamble Latin America, demonstrated the financial value of honoring participants' motivations. Faced with new equipment that was producing inconsistent results at three sites, Eduardo went to work. "To get cooperation from key manufacturing colleagues, we concentrated on their individual motivations."

Eduardo asked his teammates questions that revealed their pride, values and how they wanted to be perceived by the rest of the organization. He said: "We would have never known these motivations if we hadn't asked. This provided the foundation for a step change in technology that is enabling P&G to avoid capital equipment expenses of up to $2 million over the next five years."

CHAPTER 17

Getting the Elephant Off Your Career Track

Becoming an Expert at Leading Efforts for Change

Leadership, like any other skill, takes practice. Developing new habits necessitates dissolving old ones. A mid-level manager in a pharmaceutical company said, "I was so accustomed to the old approach of making all the decisions, telling people what to do, and devising tricks to motivate them that I had actually become a bit hardened.

"I'd spent my entire career blaming poor results on my team instead of examining the approach I was using.

"The 3 Conditions That Support Change paralyzed me at first. I kept wishing for a magic wand. This is leadership that requires effort. But the big payoff came. Last week, a guy who

107

has worked for me for fourteen years told me at the end of a conversation that, for the first time in our history, he trusted me. Wow. What's that worth?"

Trust—with its companions, bonding and support—helps make organizations immune to elephants. Trust provides a foundation for the Wellness Culture that allows a team or a family to withstand the storms of doubt, indecision, failure and stress. The average person, in an effort to develop this priceless quality, demands or asks others to trust him. The skilled leader goes upstream and honors the 3 Conditions That Support Change, knowing trust will be a natural by-product of using the tool.

With whom and in what situations can you build greater trust by placing more emphasis on the 3 Conditions That Support Change?

But Honoring the 3 Conditions Takes Time—Or Does It?

Research shows that, on average, CEOs spend less than four years in their positions within the organization. Because of their responsibilities to shareholders, and because time is so short, can anyone in the organization afford to honor the 3 Conditions That Support Change?

To some unaccustomed to using this tool, it may appear that acknowledging people's contributions, asking questions, co-creating objectives and execution plans, and discovering motivations takes more time than telling people what to do and demanding certain results.

Obviously, telling a person what to do takes less time than asking a question—initially. Yet every reader knows what takes place in the shadow of this tired leadership approach: all the things that cost leaders their jobs, including short-term problems such as disengagement and poor performance. But the long-term costs are even more devastating: costly rework, employee turnover and dissatisfied customers.

It may take more time to honor the 3 Conditions That Support Change up front, but leaders who have mastered this approach realize they have *more* time downstream.

"Real change doesn't happen from the top down anyway," says Barbara Cogan of Heska Corporation. "It only happens when it bubbles up from employees and is owned by them, and then is confirmed by those at the top. Real change occurs when employees reap the benefits themselves. The 3 Conditions That Support Change—developing people, gaining their ideas and using their motivations—ensures all that."

Tom Mariani, a regional finance officer for Navistar Financial Corporation in Schaumburg, Illinois, demonstrates what Barbara is talking about. "I took over a position another person had held successfully for many years. The team was used to business as usual with the other leader. Changes had to be made, and I was concerned that breaking habits might be difficult.

"But in response to the 3 Conditions That Support Change, we've seen greater ownership. We started by looking at our successes. [*Participants in the change process feel good about themselves.*] I stated our new goals as I saw them, and next we all discussed how to get there. [*The process includes participants' ideas.*] Then we moved to considering the changes that were in store for us. The employees were the ones who brought up issues like pay and work hours and came up with creative ideas to make the changes work for everyone. [*The process includes participants' motivations.*]

"Ultimately, we came away with a solid game plan that was based on their ideas and motivations. People are genuinely excited and enthusiastic. This is more than I could have wished for had I relied on leadership without using this tool."

Nearly two years later, Tom Mariani reported that the application of the 3 Conditions That Support Change and other leadership technology described in this book are having a positive effect on results. "We are up forty percent over last year in acquisitions and are on track to achieve both our acquisition goal and our yield goal—usually mutually exclusive in today's market—for the first time in five-plus years. We are going to exceed $1 billion in retail-lease receivables for the first time in five-plus years. Our portfolio is the best in the country." And to top it off, he added: "We just completed an employee survey where ninety-five percent indicated they are very happy with their jobs and work environment. It has truly been a team effort."

Tom, along with other leaders, is demonstrating the difference between demanding or hoping for change versus using leadership technology to make change happen, all while developing a Wellness Culture.

 What is your plan for becoming more intentional, and more successful, at creating change?

Part Four

ELEPHANT-FREE DECISION MAKING

*Consider the possibility that we are
constantly training those around us
how to act, how to behave . . .*

CHAPTER 18

A Wellness Culture Tool: The Magic Moment

When Leadership Happens

Imagine you are about to start the monthly planning meeting. You sit there, waiting, tapping your fingers. Finally, nearly ten minutes after the starting time, the remaining members of the team straggle in. Their tardiness is frustrating, inexcusable. *Have they no respect?* You start the meeting through gritted teeth.

Almost immediately, your finance person says that he doesn't have the numbers. He carries on about some excuse or another, but you cannot even hear him.

Don't have the numbers? Don't have the numbers! You've known about this meeting for weeks and you're still not prepared? You reach for the roll of antacids in your pocket to keep from erupting out loud.

What would you do in this situation? What leadership tool would you employ?

Even when you live and work in a Wellness Culture, even if there are no elephants in your office, no one can predict what is going to happen next. If we do not know how the events of a day will unfold, if we cannot see into the future, when does leadership happen?

Answer: It happens at the Magic Moment.

A Magic Moment is any time we receive information and face a choice—a choice in determining what actions we will take and what we will say.

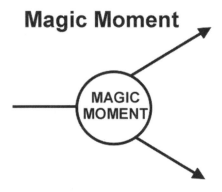

In working with business people around the world, we have conducted research which shows that just over half of us will say or do something destructive when faced with a situation like the "missing numbers" one above. At that critical point, in that Magic Moment when people discover that things have not gone the way they wanted them to, their words and body language lash out with harmful messages.

Another large group of people do nothing. They simply ignore the situation.

These two types of leaders miss the most important decisions that take place during a day. When missed, these Magic Moments, which number in the thousands, breed and feed office elephants.

But other people seize such Magic Moments and use them in their favor. Life happens. (Read: Competition happens, market conditions happen, personnel and supplier issues happen, and so forth.) These leaders recognize an opportunity and leverage the moment to deliver results now—*and guarantee greater results in the future*. This is elephant-free decision making.

Determining an organizational strategy is the easy part. Success is determined in the countless decisions made each day as that strategy is executed. To what extent are such decisions in your organization elephant-free?

Why are some people more adept at being proactive throughout the day rather than destroying immediate and long-term results by being reactive? A select group of people have found the key: They know they always have the freedom to choose their thoughts, words and actions.

**These people recognize the pivotal moments
when they have the opportunity to choose
how they want to interact with others.
They understand that no matter what choice
they make, it will bring consequences.
That moment of choice is called
the Magic Moment.**

The Magic Moment is a leadership moment. It is a point at which a person has the opportunity to choose between actions. These may be actions that achieve results in the short term but hurt individuals, relationships, culture and results in the long term. Or they may be actions that get results in the short term *and* long term by developing people, relationships, and a Wellness Culture.

A person who does not pause, who does not recognize a Magic Moment, is a blind person. People who do not use Magic Moments to improve conditions for themselves and others are people who can only react to what is happening. They live in a world of outcomes and limit results and potential.

In contrast, people who take advantage of Magic Moments literally ensure a stronger future for themselves, their organizations and humanity. Such people see Magic Moments as a priceless gift. They know that they can never fully determine the circumstances in their lives, but they can always determine their reactions to the circumstances. They make those choices during Magic Moments.

The Elephant-Free Home:
A Magic Moment That Hits Home

"Mornings around our house are probably like mornings in a lot of other homes," one man told us. "It's like a storm. We're all running around in fifth gear, and I'm shouting, 'Where's your homework? You need your coat. Grab your lunch!' and 'Mary, leave Michael alone!'

"At the same time, I'm trying to get my own stuff together. At some point, there's always that sinking feeling: I'm not going to get those e-mails finished. In fact, I'll be lucky if I make it to the office for my first meeting." His voice amped up as he continued. "So then I step up the tempo. 'C'mon, kids! You're gonna make me late.' I rush past my wife, throw her a kiss, and then sprint out the door.

"But there's another roadblock: The windows on the car are iced over. I curse under my breath, making sure

(continued on next page)

The Elephant-Free Home:
A Magic Moment That Hits Home
(continued)

Michael, who's right behind me, doesn't hear. I throw my things in the car, start the engine and attempt to scrape the windows."

He sat back and threw up his arms. "That's when Mary comes out of the house without her coat. 'Mary! Go get your coat!' I yell at her. 'But Daaaaaad,' she whines. I cut her off in a hurry: 'Don't "Dad" me! Go get your coat *now*!'

"By the time we're on the road, everyone is cranky, except Michael, who breaks the silence.

"'Dad?'

"'Yes, Michael?'

"'I forgot my lunch.'

"This is when I lose it. '*Michael! Doggone it!*' I turn the car around. 'How could you forget your lunch! I told you to grab it! Now I'm definitely going to be late. And you're going to be late too.' My hands are squeezing the plastic off the steering wheel. 'Don't expect me to write you a note. You can explain to Mrs. Simms yourself why you're late.' I hit the wheel with my fist. 'Damn it, Michael!'"

The father's shoulders dropped as he exhaled. "I've missed more Magic Moments than I care to remember. Looking back, I should never have been surprised by what happened a couple of weeks later when I picked Michael up at school. The school secretary met me at the door and said they needed money for Michael's lunch that day. I paid her but thought this was odd;

(continued on next page)

The Elephant-Free Home:
A Magic Moment That Hits Home
(continued)

Michael always brought his lunch from home.

"When we got to the car, I said to Michael, 'I had to pay the secretary for your lunch today, son. What happened?'

"Michael looked down and said, 'I forgot my lunch.'

"Without thinking, I asked, 'Well, why didn't you tell me?'

"It will take a long time to forget the look Michael gave me as he choked out, 'I tried.'"

Consider the possibility that we are constantly training those around us how to act, how to behave, simply by how we use the Magic Moment.

CHAPTER 19

The High Road And the Low Road

This Is How You Break Leadership Lock

Breaking Leadership Lock so we can deliver better results means making better decisions about how we operate personally and how we interact with others. The concept of the High Road and the Low Road has been around for centuries.

By definition, a leader who is concerned with fixing and resolving a situation in the present moment with little or no regard for developing people, relationships and results into the future is taking the Low Road.

Signs and actions on the Low Road include:

- Withholding information that would be helpful to someone else.

- Micromanaging rather than fully trusting another person.

- Ignoring performance issues.

119

- Believing that someone does not want to be great.

- Trying to fix people rather than develop them.

- Excluding others from decision making.

- Forcing our motivations onto others.

When Michael's father discovered that Michael had forgotten his lunch, he handled the moment of choice—the Magic Moment—in a way that conveyed the message that his son was bad and needed fixing. He handled the immediate situation but left these long-term consequences:

- Michael received the message "I am not capable" from his father. This sets him up for a future of failures because of an inaccurate belief system.

- Michael did not learn new, broader strategies for thinking ahead and being accountable for his own needs.

- The relationship between the two was tortured instead of nurtured.

As a person committed to fostering a Wellness Culture, how would you respond to Michael's declaration that he had forgotten his lunch? What firm, direct words would you use to make sure he realized his failure to remember his lunch had consequences and you considered it important for him to remember his lunch in the future? How would you convey all this in a way that would strengthen the relationship between the two of you?

The Low Road is a circus road. More than elephants parade into offices and homes when people choose the Low Road. They are likely to experience poisonous snakes, spitting monkeys and animals of prey along the Low Road as well. Taking advantage of Magic Moments is important; otherwise, we are victims of our own responses.

If we all know what the Low Road looks like, what do wellness leaders do to ensure a different approach?

The Wellness Culture Leadership Choice: The High Road

Do you know someone who is able to maintain a sense of calm even during stressful, chaotic times? People like this are so strong in their awareness that they can differentiate and separate their thoughts, feelings and actions.

By definition, High Road leaders make developing people and relationships an equal priority with handling the current situation and delivering results.

They do that by asking this sort of question: How can I best create strong short-term and long-term results and move the relationship with this person forward?

Signs and actions of the High Road include:

- Assisting others, regardless of what they have or have not done for us.

- Asking others for their ideas.

- Addressing tough issues directly.

- Remaining non-defensive in the face of accusatory or derogatory comments.

- Keeping the team objective rather than personal positioning or gain as the priority.

- Showing true interest in others, tapping into what is important to them.

- Giving credit to others when they deserve it.

- Developing people rather than trying to fix them.

Low Road leaders may argue that taking the High Road in some situations means we condone the current behavior or outcome. Nothing is further from the truth.

High Road leaders know that they can be very direct—saying no if necessary—and still develop people and results. These people make choices to ensure an elephant-free future.

Taking the High Road to More Pay

Curt, the owner and president of a service company in Denver, Colorado, is a wise boss who saw the effects on his bottom line when he used a Magic Moment to choose the High Road.

Much to Curt's disappointment, he received a two-week notice from Jevon, his lead salesperson. Jevon's percentage of the company's sales was so great that his loss meant extreme risk for the company.

Curt was angry. Two weeks was not enough time to hire and train another salesperson. He had repeatedly asked his employees for the courtesy of communication, especially that they inform him the moment they began to look for another job so he could make plans for a replacement. If employees gave him this courtesy, he gave them the courtesy of paid days off to interview for another job.

Everyone in the company could sense the impending meltdown. In his rage, Curt began to identify ways he could penalize Jevon and withhold his pay. Meanwhile, Jevon slid into despair.

His closing ratio had fallen in recent months as he mulled over the decision to leave the company. Now, with Curt upset, it took everything Jevon had just to show up for work.

Two days after he submitted his notice, payday arrived for everyone but him. He had submitted his numbers to figure his commission, but the paycheck did not come. "I wasn't totally surprised," Jevon said. "I'd heard Curt was considering penalizing me for what I thought were unrelated events, but frankly, I was too exhausted to fight him over it."

Instead, Jevon took a Magic Moment, sat down, and wrote an e-mail to his boss expressing his desire to end their four-year relationship in a better way. He wrote that he would like to be paid in full for the systems he had sold but said he was willing to give up the commission on any of his sales that were installed after his departure. "It was my way of waving the white flag," Jevon said.

Meanwhile, Curt was taking his own Magic Moment. "First, it occurred to me that my anger was doing no good," he said. "I realized any decisions I made in such an angry state would be based on emotion, and that's no way to lead. I also realized I had to come up with a way to move systems during the absence of a lead salesperson."

Curt's solution surprised him. "Because I was no longer angry, I could think long term. That's when it dawned on me how much I needed Jevon to perform during his last two weeks on the job. Like a slap in the face, I realized that by taking the Low Road, by penalizing Jevon and speaking poorly of him to the rest of the team, I was minimizing the chance that he'd perform well. *I* was the one with the greatest influence on Jevon's productivity.

"When I received his e-mail, I knew what I had to do. Not only would he be compensated fully but I would also make sure he understood he would be paid for every system he sold—even those installed after his departure."

The results of Curt's Magic Moment and subsequent High Road actions were apparent immediately. "It was an incredible gift," Jevon said. "I had to relocate for the new job I had gotten, so every penny counted. Curt could have made my life miserable; instead, I felt that he was saying thank-you for the years I had given the company. Just talking about this is an incredible rush!" Jevon said.

Buoyed by a new spirit, Jevon approached his final two weeks of work with renewed vigor. Over the last twelve days his closing percentage went up 43 percent, and his contract value rose by 18 percent.

By paying attention to a Magic Moment, which allowed him to think long term and take the High Road, Curt secured the stability his company needed to overcome the temporary vacancy in the lead sales position. The amount Curt paid Jevon over those two weeks was minuscule compared with what an underperforming salesperson would have cost the company in lost revenue.

CHAPTER 20

Plug In Leadership Tools Here

Intentional Actions Allow You to Be Who You Want to Be

The Magic Moment that comes before every turn onto the High Road is the point at which wellness leaders pause and plug in their leadership tools of choice. Rather than simply willing themselves to take the High Road, wellness leaders use powerful questions to guide themselves and others to higher ground.

- How can I respond to this situation in a way that builds rapport?

- What actions can I or we take to resolve this situation without creating more work for us later?

- What can I say in a firm, direct way to make my expectations clear?

- What questions can I ask to honor the 3 Conditions That Support Change?

- How can I elicit greater results from this person without micromanaging or controlling?

- How can I communicate so that this person knows I know he wants to be great?

What is the value of taking the High Road? One training participant answered, "I've been looking for a way to keep people motivated to achieve difficult objectives during an economic downturn and in a tough competitive environment.

"Taking the High Road has helped us to think carefully before responding to negative reports and to look for ways to improve rather than dwelling on the negative."

The result? "People have reacted positively," he said. "They feel less threatened and more willing to stretch."

"You can have cutting-edge technology, focus on lean manufacturing and use all the quality and efficiency practices," said Paul Curtis, vice president for manufacturing for Caraustar Custom Packaging. "You can have generous funding and the best marketing wizardry known, but a leader who doesn't understand and use this simple tool—the Magic Moment—will never achieve exceptional results. Leadership is like technology. Unless it's applied appropriately at the right times, it's nearly useless."

A recent graduate of a Wellness Culture training program described how, in an effort to take the High Road, she plugged two Wellness Culture tools into a Magic Moment that many organizations currently face.

She said, "We were formulating a strategy to provide an incentive bonus to employees and changing the structure of profit-sharing payments to reduce costs. This strategy involved human resources, finance and the tax folks, all of whom have different goals and objectives. By using the 3 Conditions That Support Change and staying on the High Road, we were able to arrive at a decision that satisfied all the parties' objectives. As a result, the company will likely save $2 million per year without any negative effect on employees."

That is a significant result. But there is another outcome that will give this person's organization exponential returns long into the future. Because of *how* the company's leaders did business, this leader reported that the process "built a strong sense of respect and team feeling."

 How would using the Magic Moment just 10 percent more each day allow you to move forward in your area of Leadership Lock?

Desired outcomes are not the result of random acts. Organizations that are ridding themselves of elephants and building Wellness Cultures are not leaving their work environments to chance.

These organizations' leaders are making deliberate choices. They know the Magic Moment is when leadership happens. If we are unable or unwilling to take advantage of Magic Moments, we can throw away all our leadership books and seminar registrations. If we do not use this one leadership tool, none of the other tools will work.

What is the key to recognizing those vital moments? It is something we all have, but not everyone uses.

CHAPTER 21

A Wellness Culture Tool: The Awareness Muscle

Flex Your Awareness Muscle and Become a Better Leader

After observing thousands of leaders worldwide, we have concluded that the biggest factor separating good leaders from extraordinary ones is the ability to use the Magic Moment.

How do they do it? How do they, moment after leadership moment, capitalize on the Magic Moment? Whenever we ask this question the answer is clear: "You have to be aware of the moments."

Your Awareness Muscle is your ability to recognize and assess your thoughts and external information to an extent that allows you to adjust your behavior.

Daniel Goleman's book *Primal Leadership: Learning to Lead with Emotional Intelligence* (Harvard Business School

Press, 2002) highlights his research showing that awareness is the mother of all emotional growth, including a person's development as a leader. In other words, the stronger our Awareness Muscles are, the more Magic Moments we can capitalize on.

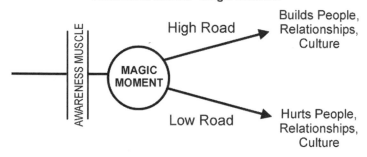

As you consider the strength of your Awareness Muscle, try this fitness test:

- How many Magic Moments do you recognize in a typical day?

- In heated moments, how strong is your ability to use the Magic Moment for the long-term benefit of everyone involved?

- Are your thoughts of real information or imagined information? Are your thoughts healthy or unhealthy?

- How would you rate your effectiveness at pausing, identifying the course of action that would elicit the best short- and long-term results, and then applying the appropriate leadership tool?

- How closely is your future success as a leader—and your effectiveness as a friend and family member—tied to your ability to increase your awareness?

All the leadership tools we have will not do us any good if we cannot call on and implement them. It all begins with the Awareness Muscle.

What Condition Is Your Awareness Muscle In?

Each of us has an Awareness Muscle, so to varying degrees, we are all able to use Magic Moments effectively. Yet significant numbers of people pay little attention to developing their Awareness Muscles. You have observed these people trudging through life in a numbed-out state, unaware that they could choose a different way to live. These are people who do not consciously adopt new thoughts and behaviors or use tools to live in a state of peak effectiveness or on a roll. Their Awareness Muscles are flabby.

How often have you heard someone say, "Oh shoot, it's going to be one of those days"? A wellness leader can easily translate these words: This person will allow external events to determine the quality of his day. This person does not realize he has another choice. His Awareness Muscle is flabby.

The Top Ten Signs of a Flabby Awareness Muscle

1. Feels like a victim, frequently saying, "Ah, #$&*! This is going to be one of those days."

2. Claims life is all about choices but constantly complains about the circumstances of his life.

3. Believes others in his family must change before he can be excited about anything again.

4. Kicks himself for the stupid things he did during the day.

5. Wishes things were different from the way they are at the moment.

6. Compares himself either too favorably or too unfavorably with others.

7. Blames the fact that he cannot get anything done due to the circumstances in his life.

8. Feels sorry for himself.

9. Focuses on one list: everything that has not gotten done.

10. Shortchanges himself on sleep, healthy food and exercise.

People who live elephant-free lives consistently evolve. Their Awareness Muscles are so strong that they can occasionally see Magic Moments before they occur. These are the people who truly shape the future.

The Awareness Muscle Workout

You are flexing your Awareness Muscle right now. We were exercising ours as we wrote this. People flex their Awareness Muscles each time they:

- Assess their responses to past situations.

- Observe their internal thought processes and adjust if necessary.

- Remember they have choices about how they respond to events.

The degree to which we reflect on these considerations determines whether we are developing our Awareness Muscles, simply maintaining them or allowing them to deteriorate.

Rodrigo Bustamante, quality manager at the Ford Motor Company stamping and assembly plant in Hermosillo, Mexico, stresses the subtle but powerful difference this muscle makes. "The Awareness Muscle is necessary not only to identify the Magic Moment but also to overcome the comfort of choosing what can often seem the easier way, the Low Road."

How will developing your Awareness Muscle strengthen your ability to unlock your leadership in moments when time seems more important than ethics or when results appear more important than people?

Developing Your Awareness Muscle in a Wellness Culture

Office elephants prey on cultures where Awareness Muscles are weak. In such environments, people often become critical of management and those around them, demonstrating their own weak Awareness Muscles.

Conversely, people who find themselves in less than ideal situations can have a completely different response. They know that while their Awareness Muscles may have to work extra hard, such environments present incredible opportunities for their personal growth and leadership. "Using my Awareness Muscle to recognize the Magic Moment allowed me to look at a criticism in a positive way and to value the knowledge of the whole team," said an employee of a carton manufacturing plant in Chicago. "This resulted in rapid, effective solutions that impressed our customers and demonstrated the professional nature and Wellness Culture our plant enjoys."

Organizations with Wellness Cultures know that the success of the bottom line is a function of the cumulative choices made in millions of Magic Moments.

One of the most important things an organization can do is help its employees build their Awareness Muscles. This leads to better decision making. Are the muscles in your organization or family bruised from repeated Low Road altercations or bulging from High Road events?

To build the Awareness Muscle, wellness leaders ask powerful questions before, during and after challenging situations. These questions demonstrate what an Awareness Muscle workout looks like in action:

- What are our thoughts regarding this person, event or situation?

- What thoughts do we want to have regarding this person, event or situation that will help move this forward?

- What actions can we take to achieve greater long-term results?

- What can we do to be at our best right now and when this situation or similar ones occur in the future?

- Why is it important for us to take the High Road in handling this interaction, event or situation?

The Moment to Deliver Something Extraordinary

Now is the only time to change. "Now" has also proven to be the most difficult time to change. Many people lament missed opportunities to do something different in the past. Others claim they will change in the future. Both miss the only time to do something: now.

As our Awareness Muscles grow, important things happen. We increase our ability to accomplish what we know we can achieve, to live according to our principles and values. We boost our ability to be the people we know we can be.

For those who have already read the Humanity Factor, the final part of this book, you know the importance of the above. You know that, as individuals, we have tremendous opportunities each day to make a difference in our lives and the lives of others. You know that each Magic Moment is an opportunity to deliver something extraordinary.

Imagine living a life where you had to rely on events—a wedding, a certain job, or for someone to act in a certain way—before you could live according to your own principles and values. Such an approach is one that ignores or brushes aside Magic Moments. People who live this way are the ones who later say, "I wish I would have . . ."

Many people who read these chapters on the Awareness Muscle, Magic Moments, and the High Road see immediately what is possible. These are people who, during interactions, see the whole person in others.

For example, when in meetings with colleagues, they are not focused on trying to manipulate others into doing something. Instead, they see colleagues as people with strengths, desires, their own values, their own families and their own issues. They know that they are in partnership with these people, and so they use the meetings to move those people, the relationships and the business forward.

These leaders use Magic Moments to deliver the Humanity Factor to others as well as to themselves.

Rosario Lopez, an administrator in quality assurance at Procter & Gamble in Mexico, is one of these people. "In taking a close look at myself, I realized my actions were causing the troubles I was having with money and work and my life.

At that moment, I decided to take control by building my Awareness Muscle and using Magic Moments.

"It sounds simple, but instantly I started feeling like a better person. I immediately began to see more efficiency and productivity in my life, and a greater focus on what is really important."

The added strength to Rosario's Awareness Muscle came just in time. She said, "After three years of not communicating with my father, I finally was able to move to a state of accepting and understanding him. I found myself becoming more humble. The gift in this was important. My father passed away just weeks after we were able to reconnect. I am left with peace of mind and gratitude."

People like Rosario and others who bring this approach to life have such strong Awareness Muscles that they leverage and use Magic Moments in extraordinary ways. The world's Wellness Culture relies on these people for its very existence.

Part Five

ELEPHANT-FREE THINKING

Your ability to unlock your leadership and keep elephants out of the office has everything to do with focus.

CHAPTER 22

A Wellness Culture Tool: The 3 Mind Factors

How You Apply What You Know Makes the Difference

Any two people who have the same IQ can still be very different in ways that have nothing to do with their intelligence. One might be capable of moving forward—being productive, enjoyable to be around and in control—while the other may present entirely different characteristics.

Abundant research demonstrates that EQ, the ability to manage one's emotions, is equally important as IQ to success. Still, all of us know people who have tremendous EQs and IQs but whose lives go in circles and whose results are average. There has to be more to determining how successful a person will be.

What determines how any person moves beyond both intelligence and emotional control to the larger issue of how he manifests himself in the real world? The answer lies in exactly how the human mind works—a topic of a large and growing body of research.

Consider how important knowing how your mind works might be.

- What would you be able to accomplish if you managed your thoughts more effectively—rather than allowing your thoughts to manage you—so that you could more fully use your intellect, emotional intelligence and wisdom?

- How would having greater control of your thoughts enhance your ability to take advantage of Magic Moments, move things forward in relation to your Leadership Lock and develop the culture around you?

- What advantage would it give you to know that the way we use our minds to navigate information and organize our thoughts could be distilled into three proven, easily applicable principles?

Three such principles make up the Wellness Culture tool called the 3 Mind Factors. The 3 Mind Factors are nothing revolutionary; in fact, each person on the planet uses them at every moment. The difference lies in *how* people use them.

Let us see what these look like in action.

The 3 Mind Factors

1. We can only focus on one thing at a time.
2. The mind cannot avoid a "don't."
3. We go toward what we focus on.

A Case Study:
Two Friends—Same World, Different Results

Amy:
Amy slipped her arms into the jacket of her blue business suit as she considered the day ahead. *The board will be in today; the public allegations are serious. It's time we learned some valuable lessons. And if we do this right, maybe we can even improve our public image.* Another thought came rushing in. *Oh shoot! The Johnson proposal is now a week late. I need some help on this. But Sid can't seem to—.* She stopped and sat up straight. *It's time to be crystal clear in my communication with him.*

Catherine:
Across town, Catherine slipped her arms into the jacket of her dark brown business suit as thoughts of the day ahead began to pile up in her head. *No doubt the auditors will choose today for their inspection. Corporate is so clueless.* Another thought came rushing in. *Oh rats! There's no way I'm going to get the Edwards bid completed today. Well, forget it. If no one else is worried about getting it done, why should I sweat it?*

Amy:
Amy got to the office five minutes later than she had intended. A coffee spill during her commute had caused a bit of excitement. "You're going to love the story behind this," she exclaimed, laughing with her colleagues as they greeted each other.

Amy's first stop was her supervisor's office. Ben was not exactly the approachable type, but Amy was not one to sit around and play the victim.

Inside Ben's large, plush office, the two of them exchanged thoughts regarding the board's visit. Then Amy said, "As a site, we've got an opportunity to learn some lessons from this, Ben. And if we handle things right, we can even sharpen our image a bit."

"How do you propose we do that?" Ben asked, raking his fingers through his graying hair.

"We put together a team, a proactive team, to identify the most important things we can learn, the steps we need to take to move forward, and how we hold ourselves accountable."

Ben tapped his pen against his mahogany desk. "All right. You put the team together and map out your intentions so we can deliver our plan to the board this afternoon."

Amy shut the office door behind her. *This afternoon! I'm already swamped.* She paused in the hallway. *There are more fires raging around here than stars in the sky.* She started walking to her cube and then picked up speed. *But if this committee comes up with a good plan, a bunch of these fires will put themselves out.*

Catherine:

Catherine got to the office five minutes later than she had intended. A coffee spill during her commute had guaranteed a lousy day and signaled that others should stay clear. Her colleagues parted like the Red Sea as she walked to her cube.

She was just sitting down when Phil, her supervisor, appeared. "Odds are the auditors will make this their week," he said calmly.

Catherine turned and glared at him. "Hey, I'm not going to change my dance just 'cause they're sniffing around. Corporate has never trusted us, so why should we make things easier for them?"

Phil stood silently for a moment, and then offered, "Perhaps, but I'd like you to put together a team so we can work with these number folks—"

"Work with them?" Catherine cut him off. "Phil, I'm up to my neck around here. The auditors will have a to-do list a mile long. Let's not give them more ammunition by offering to help. Besides, what sort of message does that send? We're guilty?"

Phil shrugged his shoulders and walked away. "I can't believe that guy," Catherine muttered to herself. She picked up the phone and dialed Sam's extension. It rang once.

"This is Sam."

"Sam. Catherine. Listen to me. The Edwards bid is due at five. Tell the team I'm not interested in any of their excuses. If they can't get it done by five, then I expect them to do whatever it takes to have it on my desk before my coffee gets here in the morning." She paused. "Don't let the team get distracted, Sam. Don't take no for an answer. And don't go in with your wimpy 'we'll do our best' attitude. If this bid doesn't get done, we'll all pay. Clear?"

A moment of silence followed. Then Sam said softly, "Aye-aye, Captain."

"Good." Ignoring his sarcasm, Catherine hung up the phone. But the crisis was not over. She gritted her teeth, knowing she would have to check on the team's progress at least twice, if not more. *I'll never get the audit work done,* she thought to herself.

Amy:
Fresh from Ben's office, Amy settled into her chair, picked up the phone and dialed an extension. It rang once.

"This is Sid."

"Sid, this is Amy. Do you have a second? I've got something to cover that's pretty important."

There was a slight pause, then, "It's crazy down here, Amy."

Amy took a deep breath. "I know, Sid, but the Johnson proposal is now a week late. On top of that, we've got the board's visit today, and I'm going to lead our efforts with them." She stopped. She was about to tell Sid what to do, but suddenly she remembered a better way to elicit Sid's help. She took a deep breath and continued. "Sid, it's imperative that the Johnson document be delivered first thing tomorrow. Because of my work with the board, I have to have more of your help with the Johnson project."

Silence filled Amy's ear. Finally, Sid replied, "I've tried to get the others to move, Amy, but everyone's swamped."

"Then it's time to be very clear in your expectations. Tell them what the priorities are, then ask them how they can make it happen." She wondered if Sid realized she was modeling the behavior she wanted him to exhibit.

"So, Sid, what steps will have to be taken today to fill in the gaps on the proposal?"

To Amy's surprise, she got an immediate and clear response. She followed with another question. "What are your ideas for getting follow-through from the team?"

Another solid answer. Amy realized that Sid knew his colleagues better than she thought.

Concerned about execution, she asked, "Do you anticipate any stumbling blocks today, and if so, what can we do in advance to head them off?"

After giving the question some thought, Sid said, "I think we should do some resource planning."

Amy thanked Sid and told him she admired how he planned to include the team in the process. She made a mental note to follow up in the afternoon by acknowledging the team's progress and asking additional questions.

Perfect, she thought. *This gives me the time I need to get ready for the board.*

Catherine and Amy:
Catherine and Amy had been getting together for dinner the first Monday of each month since they graduated from college. They called this ritual their sanity check. Amy was already at their table when Catherine slowly walked in. "I need a drink," she said, slumping into her seat.

Amy's smile disappeared. She had quit thinking about work and was eager to swap updates about boyfriends. But Catherine looked as if she had been through a war and was going to drag the day into the night—again.

"Don't tell me," Catherine said, shoving her scarf in her bag. "You had another one of your terrific days, right?"

Amy shrugged her shoulders and then realized it was time for some straight talk. She cared too much about Catherine to remain silent. "Yes, I did." She paused and then added, "Because I chose to."

Catherine lifted her eyebrows and chuckled. "Oh good. It's time for another of your 'choosing our attitude' speeches." She stopped herself as she attempted a smile. "Amy, I know it's my choice. But when I'm unable to deliver on that choice, it makes things worse."

She sighed. "Conceptually, I get it." She held up her hand and tallied her thoughts. "Choose your attitude. Empower people. Create and stick to a vision. Ask questions. I understand all that."

She held up her other hand and began to count. "I understand that I have to include them. That they should enjoy their jobs if I'm going to get results. That we should have great communication and trust and momentum."

She put her hands back in her lap. "And I understand that it has to start with me. But that's just the concept. How do I *do* it?"

Focus Determines Direction— Direction Determines Success

Fact: At this moment, you are either moving backward or forward in your life. Regardless of intelligence level, past experience, emotional health, wealth or personal tastes, the way you use the 3 Mind Factors determines whether you are advancing in your life or not. The same holds true for your team and family.

Your ability to guide the focus and energy— in yourself and others—determines the direction you and others will go. It determines your effectiveness as a leader.

CHAPTER 23

Mind Factor #1: You Can Only Focus on One Thing at a Time

Are You Listening?

When you are having a conversation with another person, can you tell if he is truly listening to you? When we ask this question, the response is always a resounding **yes!** Intuitively, all of us already know this first Mind Factor: The mind can only focus on one thing at a time.

Craig Ross: "When I was younger, I believed I could read the sports section of the newspaper, watch TV and carry on a conversation with my wife—all at the same time. Inevitably, she'd become angry and protest that I never listened to her, and, without realizing it, I would chisel away another foundation block of my marriage. My wife had reason for her discontent. She, like all of us, was innately aware of this first Mind Factor: I could only focus on one thing at a time."

You Already Know You Can't Do It

Try this: Stop reading for a moment, and think of two things at the same time or try to read two pages at the same time.

Any luck? Probably not. For almost all of us, one mind = one thought at a time.

Another experiment: While you are reading the words in the next paragraph, try to think of something else that is entirely unrelated to what you are reading. Ready? Go for it.

One of two things is happening right now: Either you are focused on what you are reading, or you are missing the content because your focus is elsewhere.

You already know why this is the case—because the mind can only focus on one thing at a time. Of course, we can perform a motor skill and think of something else. We can walk, chew gum and carry on a conversation with a colleague, so long as the conversation is what we are focused on. In addition, ample research reveals that even when we are multitasking, we are forcing our minds to switch from one focus to another at lightning-like speeds.

Yet only those with strong Awareness Muscles use the fact that the mind can only focus on one thing at a time to their advantage. They do not even *try* to focus on more than one thing at a time.

Mesmerizing a Lion

Have you ever watched the lion tamer at a circus? The masters of old used a four-legged stool to keep these beasts at bay. What did the king of the jungle do when confronted with the stool? Unable to choose a course of action because of the stool's multiple focus points (the four legs of the stool), the lion sat confused and semi-paralyzed.

Does focus paralysis show up in the lives of people around you? Consider your colleagues. As the day progresses, how many of them become confused and semi-paralyzed by numerous ongoing shifts in focus resulting from e-mails, phone calls, multiple projects, deadlines and stresses at home? How many of them move from task to task with a deer-in-the-headlights look?

Our ability to move forward when we attempt to hold multiple focuses, even though such a feat is impossible, is severely limited. This ultimately has a negative impact on our ability to unlock our own leadership.

In the modern-day world, there are hundreds of number-one priorities. You do not need a researcher in a lab coat to tell you that you expend precious time and energy each time you shift your focus. Each time you turn away from a particular focus, you have to return to it at some point. Consider:

- Every time you change focus, how long does it take to get back up to speed?

- What does this cost in terms of lost energy and time?

- How does it affect the efficiency of an individual or a team?

- How does it affect quality?

After numerous such shifts over the course of a day (week, month, career), mental and physical fatigue set in, costing companies countless dollars in reduced productivity and untapped promise. Is it possible that teams, families or individuals can think they are winning when they are losing?

A Case Study:
Time Out

When my husband, Doug, pulled out his Blackberry, he gave me that "just a quick check" smile that has begun to outnumber the "I love you" smiles. I shot back my "you're kidding me" eyes, to which he responded with his patented "whatever" shrug. But it's what he said that I think could haunt him the most: "It's not like he's going to get in the game or anything." And his thumbs typed on.

Doug was talking about our son. I've often wondered if Jason knows his father is not paying attention at his games. My girlfriends think I'm crazy to imagine that he doesn't. Maybe it's just my wishful thinking. Perhaps it's my hope that he won't notice. Because with that awareness, what comes next?

When Doug pointed at his handheld addiction and said, "Regional VP wants me to call in with the numbers—it'll just take me a sec," I lost it. I leaned toward his ear and shouted a whisper. "Jeez, Doug! It's your son's final home game. And what the hell is your stupid VP going to do with the numbers at eight-thirty on a Friday night anyway!"

Not a very High Road thing to say, I know. Perhaps that's why he ignored me. In a leap, he zigzagged down the bleachers, past the other parents (who apparently have normal jobs) and out the door.

I swear it happened the moment he left the gym. As if triggered by Doug's absence, the coach got out of his chair and pointed at Jason. My son stood up. I gasped. With a jerk of the thumb, the coach sent him to the floor in the final home game of his career.

For a while, I forgot all about Doug—forgot all about where I thought he was going and the price he was paying. I stood up and cheered my son as he jogged with obvious jitters onto the floor.

Maybe it was just charity. Who knows? Coach has always been classy. Jason only played a bit over two minutes, but I could tell by watching him that they were going to be the greatest two minutes of his senior year.

When the coach brought him out, the smile on Jason's face was one every mother covets. Then, with a quick glance just before he took his spot on the bench, his eyes came up to me.

What hurts is I knew that look was going to come. I knew he'd look—he'd check to see if we saw, if we knew he had had his moment. I smiled, my hands gripped together, waving them vigorously just in front of me. I was praying he wouldn't see.

With just over a minute left in the game, Doug stomped up to our seat. "Greg didn't answer, so I called Jackie and gave her the numbers," he said, sitting down. Then, "Hey, this bugger of a game is closer than I thought it would be. Did I miss anything?"

I couldn't reply. I just sat there, watching Jason laugh with his teammates on the bench, as if it were a movie I didn't want to end.

And I wondered: Can the wins in business ever compensate for the losses at home?

The Truth about Stress

Wherever we serve leaders and teams, we hear people describe the fatigue they feel from the weight of their to-do lists. "My mind is full," many claim. "I'm rarely operating at my best." Or, "I can't get anything done. I feel as if I'm constantly stressed out by my to-do list."

But can a mind really be full? Logically, the answer is no. Is it possible then that the symptoms people view as indications of a full mind—fatigue, numbness, stress—are actually caused by something else?

That something else is the unconscious or conscious mismanagement of the first Mind Factor: People can only focus on one thing at a time.

As people have gained greater mastery in their ability to make themselves and those around them focus for longer periods on just one thing at a time, they report these results:

- They save time because costly rework and additional meetings are not necessary.

- Everyone becomes more efficient.

- They are more rested throughout and at the end of the day because they have not put their minds through unnecessary stress.

Leveraging Your Intelligence, Wisdom and Experience

Understanding the power of focus has immeasurable implications. Our focus can be a destructive force, or it can be the lever we use to maximize the benefits of our intelligence, wisdom and passion.

Catherine, in the case study in Chapter 22 (page 141), uses her focus in self-destructive ways.

- She focuses on the embarrassment of spilled coffee, ruining her chance to enjoy the day.

- Rather than considering the potential benefits of the visit by the auditors, she focuses on the work they will require and on an imagined message: Corporate does not trust us.

- Instead of accepting the realities associated with the auditors' visit, she fights the circumstances—a fruitless battle and a focus that dooms future success.

- Rather than taking responsibility for the tasks that must be completed, she adopts a victim's attitude, a focus that forfeits any opportunity she and her colleagues might have for finding solutions.

- Though Catherine needs Sam's effort to be successful, she focuses on all the things she does not want him to do by communicating repeated "don'ts." This ensures a weaker effort on his part, more work for herself and a poorer outcome.

These are the results she generates:

- Poorer communication and relationships with her boss, the auditors, Sam and her team.

- An elephant looming larger in her office as critical conversations are avoided and people tiptoe past her.

- Less momentum in her life. By refusing responsibility, she saps the energy and excitement from herself and her team.

- Diminished business results as she stays in Leadership Lock. Missing numerous Magic Moments, Catherine makes the Low Road a well-worn path. As a result, her team will be unable to use the auditors' visit as a resource, and she sets the company up to repeat mistakes in the future.

- An atrophying Awareness Muscle. Because she doesn't exercise her Awareness Muscle, she is unable to grow. She creates a poorer image for herself, her team and her company. This image will cost her dearly: Her boss will be less likely to consider her for job promotions, and her colleagues will consider her less trustworthy—especially when things get difficult—and will resist collaborating with her.

- Lack of flow in her life. Catherine is not on a roll. Because she views each experience as insurmountable, she is unable to deliver more and thus develops the habit of expecting less.

Amy, on the other hand, uses her focus as a productive lever.

- Spilled coffee can be embarrassing, yet Amy does not let this distract her from a greater focus—having fun and building relationships with colleagues.

- When a visit from the board is looming, Amy accepts this as what it is, sees it as a Magic Moment and focuses on learning lessons.

- Rather than focusing on the negative messages a visit from the board might imply, Amy embraces the situation and focuses on using the experience as a resource.

- Rather than playing the victim, Amy flexes her Awareness Muscle and focuses on taking responsibility and finding solutions.

- Amy knows Sid is not going to be enthusiastic about accepting more responsibility. But rather than telling him what to do and thereby creating more work for herself, she focuses on being a role model for Sid and helping him visualize the results they can create.

These are the results Amy generates:

- Enhanced communication and relationships with her boss, the board, Sid and the rest of her team.

- A barricaded elephant. Any elephant waiting at the door for an invitation into this office must continue to wait as people grow in their ability to tell the truth.

- An even stronger Awareness Muscle and greater momentum in her life. By taking responsibility, she uses her energy and excitement to her advantage rather than throwing it away.

- Better business results as she applies the keys to unlocking leadership. Because her team will use the board's visit as a resource, she sets the organization up for greater success.

- A stronger image for herself, her team and her company. This image will pay future dividends: Her boss will give her greater consideration for job promotions, and her colleagues will consider her trustworthy—even when things get difficult—and will be eager to collaborate with her.

- A life that flows. Amy is on a roll. She gets more out of each experience, is able to deliver more, and therefore expects more of herself and others.

The Costs and Benefits of Your Focus

What is your focus doing for you? In your career, do you focus on what you do not like about your job, the company you work for, and your clueless colleagues and boss? If so, you are likely to be experiencing frustration and low job satisfaction; a feeling of stagnation as others pass you by with promotions; and a lack of energy and satisfaction in life. Your ability to move forward is dangerously close to paralysis.

On the other hand, do you focus on what you like about your job, the company you work for, and the talent that surrounds you? If this is the case, you are likely to be experiencing job satisfaction; momentum in your career as a result of effective decision making and your ability to live on a roll; and energy, inspiration, and fulfillment in life.

Your ability to unlock your leadership and keep elephants out of the office has everything to do with focus.

The Difference a Change in Focus Makes

Regarding your leadership, how would you answer these focus choices?

- What developmental difference would it make for your team if individuals focused more on what members were doing well rather than focusing on their failures?

- What financial difference would it make for your organization if it focused more on serving clients and then making a profit rather than making a profit and then serving clients?

- What difference would it make in the development of your children if more focus were placed on fostering their development rather than on fixing them?

- What difference would it make in your marriage if each of you increased your focus on creating harmony and joy rather than trying to change the other person?

- What difference would it make for a nation if together we focused on building honest, productive citizens rather than on stopping crime?

So How Do I Change My Focus?

If what we focus on determines the results we create, how do we improve our ability to alter or enhance our focus?

Six Questions to Strengthen Your
Awareness Muscle and Develop a Healthier Focus

1. Am I distracted, or is my mind restful and focused?

2. What am I currently focused on?

3. Is this focus destructive or healthy and productive? Is my focus undermining my progress or enhancing my relationships with others and helping things move forward?

4. What sort of focus do I want in order to leverage my intelligence, wisdom and experience?

5. Why is a stronger, more productive focus important to me?

6. How will I ensure a healthy focus regarding this person or situation in the future?

CHAPTER 24

Mind Factor #2: The Mind Cannot Avoid a "Don't"

See, It Is Already Happening

Don't take the time to look now, but when you examine the front cover of this book, you will notice that the elephant is in a peculiar shape. It demonstrates the power of this Mind Factor. When you look at it later, you will see what we are talking about.

We all know many leaders and parents who have spent their lives telling their employees or children what not to do. Readers with strong Awareness Muscles know that every time such instructions are issued—"don't do this," "don't do that"—individual and collective focus turns to the very thing the leader or parent wants others to avoid.

So, did you do it? Did you turn to the front cover of the book and look at the elephant? You should not be ashamed—or blamed—if you did. We told you not to. Once we told you, "Don't take time to look now," one of two things happened: You took the action you were told not to take; or you did not take the action, but for a moment you focused on what you were not supposed to do.

Either way, what happened to the continuity of your attention, your ability to continue reading, to move forward? Invariably, you were interrupted. This leadership disruption permeates work and home environments and is a major cause of Leadership Lock.

Whose Idea Was It?

"Don'ts"—including "stop," "quit," and "I told you not to"—are magnets for the human mind.

A client in Tennessee credits the use of this single Mind Factor with a decrease in workplace injuries. Previously, plant supervisors focused on telling employees where *not* to put their bodies. Don't cross yellow lines. Don't place fingers on shield.

Even in such an important area as safety, these supervisors were setting the employees up for failure. By shifting the focus toward what they *wanted* employees to do—*Please stay behind yellow lines* and *Keep hands at a safe distance*—they witnessed an immediate reduction in work-related accidents and an increase in productivity.

By telling others what not to do, we actually sabotage our best intentions as leaders. The same holds true for parents. Anyone who interacts with children knows what happens when you say "don't" to a child.

Craig Ross: "Years ago, while I was doing laundry at a Laundromat, my toddler daughter reached out her hand and asked to hold the quarters to be used for the washer. Because Father knows best, I handed her a quarter and instructed: 'Don't put it in your mouth.'

"The quarter immediately went in her mouth.

"That is scary. But you know what is scarier? It was not her idea to put the quarter in her mouth—it was mine. At that moment, I realized several things that injected my Awareness Muscle with growth hormones: I was sabotaging my best efforts as a parent. I was responsible for more of my daughter's poor behavior than I had imagined. I realized that the hurtful message I was sending my daughter, by bombarding her with don'ts, was: 'I don't trust you to make good decisions.'"

Does this principle operate the same way in adults? What if, at work or at home, we have actually been leading those around us to the very actions we are trying to discourage? What if we have been distancing ourselves from the people and results we want to be closely associated with?

By repeatedly sending "don't" messages, we train others to rely on us to make decisions for them.

"Don't" Is More Than Just a Word

Those effective at developing elephant-free cultures understand that "don't" is much more than just a word. It is a style, an approach to leadership and life. "Don't" messages silently permeate many work cultures and families. The actual word "don't" is not required to take a person's focus in a counterproductive direction. This is achieved merely by the essence of what we are communicating.

Common Forms of "Don't" in the
Workplace and at Home

• "Whatever you do, never say a word about this."

• "Quit sending so many e-mails."

• "Stop beating yourself up over this."

- "Never make that mistake again."

- "We can't miss our goal or we're sunk."

- "If I ever catch you doing that again, I'll punish you."

What difference does it make when we tell others what we *want* them to do rather than what we do not want them to do?

The following list demonstrates how changing the focus leads to a more productive way of delivering the same messages.

Making a 180-Degree Turn on "Don't"

- "Please keep this information confidential."

- "We need to be more effective and efficient at using e-mail."

- "It's important that you believe in yourself."

- "Quality is of the utmost importance."

- "We must achieve our goal."

- "It's important that you behave, starting now."

As much as we would like everyone around us to be skilled, responsible, self-starting, self-disciplined, honest and accountable, they are not going to develop these qualities by being told what not to do. What is required is a leader who re-inforces these qualities in others. What is required is a leader who helps others *discover* for themselves what to do, instead of telling them what not to do.

**The Elephant-Free Home:
The Little Boys' List**

A woman named Jacki loved how this worked with her children. "We were going to my boss's house for a dinner party with our three boys, ages eleven, eight, and three. On the way there, I asked them what things they would have to do to be good kids at the party. Boy, did I get a list! One, eat all the food you take; two, pick up after yourself; three, say 'please' and 'thank you'; and, last but not least, four, say 'excuse me' after you fart or burp.

"It's definitely a little boy's list, but I got their ideas and full participation. I could have told them what not to do or just said, 'Be good at the party tonight,' and they probably wouldn't have paid any attention to me.

"By the way, they were well behaved at the party."

The Not-So-Hidden Messages of "Don't"

Telling someone "don't," "stop," "quit," or "never" contradicts the truth that people want to be great. Almost always, "don't" commands transmit only harmful messages.

Common Messages Inherent in "Don't" Statements

- I don't trust you to know or do what is right.

- You're not capable of making good decisions.

- You need me to guide you.

No Question: Sometimes You
Have to Say No

Does this mean people should never say "no," "don't," "stop," or "quit"? Absolutely not. (There, we just did it.) Weak managers—those without the ability to say no when necessary—cost organizations millions of dollars in wasted resources. This type of drain should not be tolerated. Wellness leaders have no patience for ineffectual leadership. None. Zip. Zilch.

Imagine being the parent of a preschool-age daughter. You are playing at the park, and she starts to run into the street as a big truck comes barreling toward her. Is this a good time to yell, "Hey, great job running, sweetie! Now turn it around!"

Of course not. It is time to be firm: "Stop! Don't move!"

It is imperative that leaders say no when necessary. Yet these words are effective only if a company has established clear guidelines and fully communicated its expectations to employees. For the first time, people know what you are saying no to. Wellness leaders know employees must be informed that "this *cannot* happen again" if their performance or behavior does not meet expectations.

But what happens if there is an elephant in the office? If a company has not developed a Wellness Culture, if the workplace is characterized by lack of trust, poor communication and a focus on problems rather than solutions—and in this context, the leader says no—it only compounds the damage. It feeds the elephant as communications and relationships suffer and so do the results that follow.

What might happen if the little girl in the park has been raised in an environment where she constantly hears "stop," "quit," and "don't"? It is no secret that children become masters at tuning out nagging, *no*-oriented parents. In this case, the consequences of such an approach are chilling.

How do adults respond when they have been bombarded by "don't" communications? In many cases, employees build immune systems to ensure their own survival, and the "no" becomes lost in a sea of toxicity.

People we work with in organizations around the world consistently state that there is a connection between the "don't" approach and the level of disengagement within their organizations.

In a Wellness Culture, when people trust each other, full communication is commonplace, and focusing on solutions is the traditional approach. In these cases a "no" can actually contribute something positive to individuals as well as to the culture.

Jan Zoucha, vice president of human resources for Assurity Security Group, is one of those leaders who has become an expert at using the 3 Mind Factors to create change. "I now use my 'no's' and 'don'ts' sparingly. I keep them in my pocket for those rare cases when someone has gone outside the guidelines we co-created up front. When it comes to leading others, focus is everything; a misplaced or mistimed 'no' from me can dismantle *in seconds* everything we've worked so hard to build."

CHAPTER 25

Mind Factor #3: You Go Toward Your Focus

Where Are You Going Today?

Imagine you are driving your car and notice a gorgeous sunset off to your left. It is stunning—brilliant pinks, blues and purples. As if drawn by a magnet, your eyes lock onto the unfolding spectacle.

Suddenly you hear a horn and snap your head back in the direction of the road. Horrified, you realize your car has drifted into the opposite lane.

Why the crash course in driving? You know why because you have done something similar. You know why because you have listened to an employee inventory everything he does not like about a coworker, and then you have watched their relationship deteriorate. You know why because you have a friend or relative who always points out why something will not work—and his efforts prove him right. You know why because you have seen organizations search for what is not working, and that is all they find. You know why because you have had days when all you could see is what you did not like and then watched your energy drain away and your headache pain soar.

Steven Vannoy: "Several years ago I was feeling rotten one day—overly fatigued, snarling at almost everything, and wondering why I couldn't even begin to tackle all the work on my desk. I decided to diagram my day to see where things had started to go south. I drew a long horizontal box and divided it into ten segments to represent either the hours so far in that day or ten tasks. It didn't matter which. I started marking each box with either an X for a negative outcome or an exclamation point to signal a success, a task well done.

"I was surprised to see that only three boxes had big black X's in them; the other seven sported exclamation points. But where had I put my focus all day? On the 'problem' items, while completely ignoring the 'successful.' Until I really got the concept of going toward my focus, even one X'ed box could ruin my day.

"It didn't take too many days of this experiment to realize the power of the third Mind Factor. Now I can look at a day that might have only one exclamation point showing, but if that's where I put my focus, it can negate the negatives for the rest of the day."

An employee within a client company summed it up: "I always knew the concept of a self-fulfilling prophecy was a fact. Now I understand why. We go toward our focus."

What Are You Pointing At?

Because this Mind Factor works with others just as it works with ourselves, consider: Where are you guiding the focus of those around you?

Amy and Catherine, from the case study in Chapter 22 (page 141), have comparable life circumstances; they are the same age, have the same level of education, and face similar job pressures. Both used the 3 Mind Factors. But because Amy *understands* these Mind Factors, she uses her focus to her advantage, and she, her team and her company benefit.

Many untrained managers make the same mistakes Catherine made. With worthy intentions but flawed approaches, they point out and steer their teams toward obstacles.

- "Production is down. Go find out why!"

- "Why aren't we working together efficiently?"

- "You can't trust anyone around here, because . . ."

- "We'll never get the resources to . . ."

- "We're going to have to watch out for . . ."

- "Who did this?"

Then these managers lament that "you can't find good help anymore" and "the work ethic is dead." But is that true? Is good help really impossible to find? Is the work ethic really dead? Only if the manager killed it.

Does this mean we ignore problems and tough issues? Of course not. Root-cause analysis can be destructive—or valuable. It destroys results when the focus is on what went wrong or who is to blame. Conversely, root-cause analysis is vital and effective when it is conducted with the intention of discovering what must improve and harvesting the important lessons.

Leaders understand that focus is everything; therefore, they are careful where they point their teams. They choose their words wisely for they know that their words will eliminate the unnecessary step of taking things backward. They break Leadership Lock; once they have the root cause, they use it as a starting point to improve results.

Make a 180-Degree Turn with Focus
by Asking These Questions

- "In what additional ways can we increase our productivity?"

- "How can we work together more efficiently?"

- "What ideas do you have on how we can build greater trust?"

- "Given the resources we have, how can we best move forward?"

- "What do we want to make sure happens?"

- "What lessons can we learn from this situation?"

Stuff happens. How we use the 3 Mind Factors determines what happens next.

 Leaders lead people, but first and foremost, they lead people's focus. Where are you leading the focus of those around you?

A Healthy Approach to Business

A director of manufacturing did not waste any time putting this tool to work within his organization. He said, "We had just finished discussing the 3 Mind Factors during a Wellness Culture training session when we took a break. I spent the time checking in to hear how the plant was running.

"That week our plant was launching a new materials processing system. This was a big deal that the plant had spent eighteen months preparing for. If not launched properly, the system would have severe effects on production.

"I decided to spend my break calling one of our project leaders. When she answered the phone, I asked how the launch was going. She said, 'We have some big things that are really running slick, but we have some issues as well.'

"As I heard this, a list of questions started to form in my head—all focused on what Nancy had labeled as issues. Like a bug to a light, my focus was drawn to the problems. Had we not just covered the 3 Mind Factors, I would have asked those questions. Instead, I said, 'So tell me about the stuff that is running slick.'"

The director added, "At that moment, two things became clear to me: One, the project leader was preparing to talk about the issues as well; and two, she became excited when she spoke about the things she was proud of. I could sense her excitement in the tone of her voice. My next question asked how she planned to move the challenging issues forward. Her response was powerful and positive. We ended the conversation on that high note."

The effect of this leader's ability to lead proactively, build the relationship with the project leader and address the tough issues through questions was clear. The plant newsletter covered the story:

> Operations had more than seventy customizations and new processes that changed on Monday. That's more complexity than any other plant that has switched to [the new system]. The majority of those changes occurred without problems. Still, there are some aspects that employees are working to identify and fix.

"This project was huge and there are issues we're ironing out," said [the business team leader]. "But we can't lose sight of the fact that so much went right with this launch. . . . Letting the good things motivate us to overcome the difficult situations is a healthy approach to business."

The Elephant-Free Home: Mom and Dad Knew It All Along

Wise parents foster lifelong strengths in their children by using this third Mind Factor. They tune into and focus on the behaviors they desire in their children. By maintaining this focus, they reinforce the desired behaviors, and the children develop even stronger character and skills in those areas. But this approach is not easy.

Steven Vannoy: "Early in my parenting years, I dealt with a shy daughter. Like any parent, I wanted the best for this bright, beautiful, happy little girl. But her looking and acting like a wilted wallflower wasn't in my script for her.

"I tried the fix-it approaches. I pleaded. 'Don't be so shy!' [That backfired; see the second Mind Factor.]

"I reasoned. 'You'll never have any friends if you're so shy.' [That also backfired; see the third Mind Factor.]

"Finally, my Awareness Muscle got strong enough for me to see that I needed to change my focus. So instead of my usual introduction, 'This is my shy child,' I would say, 'This is Emmy, a delightful, friendly little girl.'

"I realized my daughter would go toward her focus, and at that age her focus *followed my focus,* so I was playing a big part in causing her shyness. Here are some of the steps I took.

(continued on next page)

The Elephant-Free Home:
Mom and Dad Knew It All Along
(continued)

- I stopped calling attention to the shy behavior.

- I looked for and focused on her outgoing behavior. For instance, I noticed when she smiled and chatted with friends who were visiting.

- To reinforce this behavior, I gave her sincere, specific and selective feedback—the 3 S's of Yes—rather than hollow compliments.

- Not surprisingly, the next time friends were over, she smiled and interacted with them. The difference was noticeable.

- Later, when I was again tempted to focus on the shy behavior, I reminded myself that, like any kid, she wanted to be great and that behavior patterns do not change overnight. Although the fix-it approach—telling her not to be shy—might have made a short-term difference, the cost would have been high: It would have deeply embedded her shy belief system over the long term and eroded our relationship."

Some leaders and parents invite elephants into the office and home because they have established an unhealthy focus. Then they watch the elephants become reckless monsters as their teams and families go toward that focus.

CHAPTER 26

The 3 Mind Factors Are Always Turned On

These Factors Affect Your Future

The influence of the 3 Mind Factors is enormous. Consider the following two examples.

Example 1

Step 1: When I initially discovered the 3 Mind Factors, I was elated. They revealed an opportunity to leverage my skills, intelligence and wisdom. I was finally able to begin unlocking issues with my leadership. I was on a roll!

Step 2: With my Awareness Muscle getting stronger, I was amazed at how many Magic Moments I was seeing and how my focus was driving everything from my attitude to the results I achieved.

Step 3: Then I began to slip. I started to notice all the times I had a destructive focus.

Step 4: I started asking myself destructive questions: Why do I keep slipping into a destructive focus? What am I doing wrong? Why can't I get it right?

Step 5: Because of this harmful focus, I lost my energy, felt lethargic, and developed a care-less attitude. I didn't have the desire to make use of Magic Moments or any other leadership tool.

Because of the power of the 3 Mind Factors, we can use a growing Awareness Muscle to beat ourselves down or lift ourselves up. Step 3 in the preceding example proved to be a critical turning point, because the person used his Awareness Muscle to focus on destructive thoughts that grew larger as he moved toward them.

Example 2

Step 1: When I initially discovered the 3 Mind Factors, I was elated. They revealed an opportunity to leverage my skills, intelligence and wisdom. I was finally able to begin unlocking issues with my leadership. I was on a roll!

Step 2: With my Awareness Muscle getting stronger, I was amazed at how many Magic Moments I was seeing and how my focus was driving everything from my attitude to the results I achieved.

Step 3: Then came my biggest challenge. I noticed the temptation to focus on all the times I had a destructive focus rather than the times I had a productive focus.

Step 4: This was a Magic Moment! I paused, took a deep breath, and asked myself: In what situations have I kept a positive focus? What can I do to adopt a stronger, more productive focus? What am I already doing well? What can I do even better?

Step 5: Because of this healthy focus, I gained energy, felt motivated and developed a can-do attitude. I gained confidence in my ability to see and use future Magic Moments, and this precipitated greater results.

Wellness leaders who use the 3 Mind Factors to guide an entire group produce significant advantages for their organizations. The 3 Mind Factors make the difference between a toxic culture and a Wellness Culture; a herd of elephants in your office and an elephant-free zone; a weak bottom line and a healthy one. Like a ship that first appears on the horizon, the shift in emotional competencies starts small and then gradually grows larger until the Wellness Culture is visible to everyone, even those outside the organization.

When Tom Weber (now vice president of Core Systems) was vice president and general manager for Caraustar Custom Packaging, he said, "Some customers came to our plant for a tour. They commented that one of the reasons they love to do business with us is because there's a different feeling here. We asked what they meant. Their responses affirmed our Wellness Culture work of collectively focusing on building relationships and supporting one another. People are friendlier, and there's a real sense of teamwork, they said."

Top organizations have discovered that the critical mass created by a collection of individuals focusing forward is the greatest resource they can cultivate.

It is a resource that cannot be duplicated by their competitors. Because the people within an organization are unique, so will their synergies and the results they create be unique. This is a strategic competitive advantage that organizations covet.

How Leaders Play Hara-Kiri during Tough Times

Many companies play the 3 Mind Factors backwards. The minute the economy slows or business declines, the managers attempt to save the day by communicating fear and scarcity. "Guys, business is down this quarter; we're going to have to cut back." Or, "All indications say the economy is leveling out, so we're putting a spending freeze in place." In one company, before a Wellness Culture training, the leadership team spent hours examining the question: "Where can we stop the bleeding?"

The result? Just when the company needs the best efforts and creative ideas from their employees, they destroy the conditions that allow for peak performances. How creative are you when you feel like a loser, are stressed out and afraid?

Unwittingly, leaders of these companies have developed a toxic culture. Because we all go toward our focus, employees in situations like these act from the focus and paradigm that business is slow and perhaps their jobs are in jeopardy. This focus, of course, makes it difficult for people to feel good about themselves, thereby violating the first condition of the 3 Conditions That Support Change. All too often, these companies not only have to endure harsh market challenges but they now have to do it while their talent has become disengaged, unmotivated and is actively looking for the nearest exit.

Sadly, for these companies the future of the business is in greater peril because of what the leaders said.

Consider:

- What difference would it make if leaders, in addition to managing company finances well and being honest about current circumstances, adopted a more productive focus?

- What difference would it make if they asked their teams:

  - "How can we move this account forward and reduce costs at the same time?"

  - "In what areas have we generated momentum on which we can build?"

  - "How can we manage our resources so they can be leveraged better?"

  - "What strengths of our team can we leverage to move ahead of our competitors in times like this?"

  - "In what areas have we proven we are capable of succeeding during periods like this?"

When times are difficult, what type of leadership approach inspires you?

The Effect of the 3 Mind Factors on an Entire Organization

How influential are the 3 Mind Factors within an organization? Consider the examples offered by Wellness Culture partners in the field and described in the next few paragraphs.

Example 1

Step 1: The president stood before the entire organization, starting his speech with talk of hope, tradition and potential position in the market. (His words were met with enthusiastic applause. People leaned forward in their seats to get a better view.)

Step 2: Then the president described the mistakes of the past and their causes. "Never again will we . . ." and "We shouldn't have . . ." (This focus made people uncomfortable. They sat back in their chairs.)

Step 3: At this point, the president admonished, "Don't worry about the impending changes. Don't believe what the papers are saying." (Instantly, audience members began worrying about the changes that were coming and wondering what the papers were saying.)

Step 4: Next, in an effort to engage the audience, the president asked questions. "What are the biggest problems we face? Why would someone be afraid to succeed here?" (On command, people whispered their answers to one another, visualizing, verbalizing and reinforcing the problems the company faced and the reasons employees were afraid to succeed.)

Step 5: When the president finished, he smiled and waved proudly as the audience applauded politely. (Fear mixed with disappointment as people filed out of the auditorium. Someone whispered, "I don't trust him.")

With the best of intentions this leader unwittingly used the 3 Mind Factors to create obstacles that employees and their teams would have to overcome in the future. He separated himself and his organization from productive results by using the forum to plant the seeds of obstruction. Then he fertilized heavily.

Example 2

Step 1: The president stood before the entire organization, starting his speech with talk of hope, tradition and potential position in the market. (His words were met with enthusiastic applause. People leaned forward in their seats to get a better view.)

Step 2: Then the president referred to the challenges of the past and described how everyone, including himself, would use those experiences to shape a more successful future. "We have learned to . . ." and "We'll take greater advantage of . . ." (This focus made people feel respected for their efforts. They stayed glued to the edge of their seats.)

Step 3: At this point, the president acknowledged that, in order for the company to move forward, change would be necessary. He outlined his vision and explained why the changes were important. Then he communicated his plan to "hear your ideas, gain your perspectives and maximize your experiences." (He was interrupted by cheers.)

Step 4: Next, in an effort to engage the audience even more, the president asked questions. "Where do you see our greatest opportunity? What do you want to do to ensure everyone succeeds?" (On command, people whispered their answers to one another, visualizing, verbalizing and reinforcing the strengths of the company and the steps they could take to succeed.)

Step 5: When the president finished, he smiled and waved proudly as the crowd gave him a standing ovation. (Enthusiasm blended with confidence as audience members pressed forward to shake the president's hand. Someone shouted, "He's one of us.")

Expert leaders use every moment to build a Wellness Culture in their organizations. They know the group mentality, shaped by their collective focus, constitutes the company's energy.

How You Use the
3 Mind Factors = Your Results

Whether the skills and attitudes people bring to the game improve or deteriorate depends on how they and their leaders use the 3 Mind Factors. Wellness leaders know that the people they interact with can only focus on one thing at a time, their minds cannot avoid a "don't," and they go toward what they focus on. People who create elephant-free zones stand out because they use the 3 Mind Factors to leverage the intelligence, wisdom and experience of every person around them.

By understanding the ramifications of focus and using specific leadership tools to guide focus, these leaders move through their careers and personal lives directing themselves and others to greater results.

Part Six

ELEPHANT-FREE OPERATIONS

Problems do not happen.
Rather, events happen, and
because of a destructive focus,
the events are distinguished as problems.
Results are instantly jeopardized.

Every minute a team focuses on problems
is a minute it cannot focus on solutions.

When we have given nearly everything
we have at work, how much sense
does it make to give our families
and friends our leftovers?

CHAPTER 27

Excuse Me—
Do You Know the
Way to Leadership?

Without New Information,
You Are Guaranteed to Get Lost

If you had to go to Los Angeles for the most important meeting of your career, and drive across the city to get there, would you use a city map from 1989? Of course not. It would be crazy trying to navigate any city using an outdated map.

It seems ridiculous, but for just a moment imagine you and I visited any city with an outdated map. What would be the impact on four vital areas of our efforts—efficiency, energy, enthusiasm and results?

Consider the possibility that many of us have been using outdated maps to conduct business and live our lives. Many of us steer our thoughts and navigate through the day using outdated, even harmful criteria and information. Outdated maps have rendered some of us—our teams and our families—ineffective, destroying results and more.

Proper Use of the Energy Map
Immediately Makes You More Effective

It is time for leadership technology to move forward. Just as society is calling for the evolution of other technologies, it is demanding higher quality leadership.

Would you encourage a colleague to create a business operating system with software developed in the 1980s? You would be laughed at—or fired. Yet many of us use outmoded personal operating systems, outdated methods of managing our focus and energy, to determine our attitudes and drive our decisions.

People use obsolete thinking, archaic belief systems and outdated education to make countless decisions every day.

What if we have been making choices that are hampering our ability to move things forward, diminishing our results, and limiting our happiness? What if the way we have been leading others and ourselves is as outdated as a 1989 map of L.A.?

Imagine possessing a map that allowed you to deliver your best in each situation, that allowed you to unlock your leadership, add the Humanity Factor to everything you do, improve results, and keep elephants out of the office. Such a map exists.

CHAPTER 28

A Wellness Culture Tool: The Energy Map

Use the Ultimate Operating System to Shape Your Future

We are always expending energy. The energy we use either hurts us or helps us, moving us backward or forward. Throughout the day, we navigate events using the 3 Mind Factors. Because we go toward our focus, and our energy follows our focus, we are always headed in one direction or the other on what is called the Energy Map. People who know how to direct energy, both within themselves and others, have a distinct advantage in and out of the workplace. They create greater results.

By using the 3 Mind Factors to master focus, leaders within a culture—and that means all of us—can direct energy more effectively. The 3 Mind Factors constitute the routing mechanism for the personal operating system, the Energy Map.

As people strengthen their Awareness Muscles, they are better able to assess and align their focus. They can chart a course for the moments to come and for the long-term future in the same way they would choose a route by looking at a map.

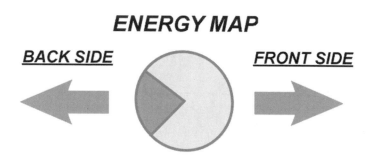

The Energy Map represents 100 percent of our energy, time and potential. It has a back side and a front side. We are always on one side or the other, moving backward or forward. We have only twenty-four hours in a day, and this map represents every second of it. We either use the time well or waste it. This operating system determines every result we generate.

The Million Dollar Meeting Club. Are You a Member?

Dan Lindberg is general manager of the Telematics Business Unit for the International Truck and Engine Corporation. This company has had its financial challenges. It would be easy for leaders to succumb to using an outdated map. But Dan and other select leaders within the organization are dedicated to upgrading the leadership operating system. Dan gave us this example: "We were told to cut $4 million from our product development budget. This was not the budget for 'wish-list programs.' This had to come from an existing program and represented 30% of our budget. This wouldn't be easy. No one thought we could do it. To make it even tougher, these results needed to be delivered quickly.

"I requested a meeting with the team. I began the meeting by asking everyone to reflect on the cost-saving successes created in the last year, and modeled this behavior with my own story. I explained why this exercise of being on the front side of the Energy Map was important. As people shared, we asked questions like 'What can the rest of us learn from that story?' and 'Where can we apply what we learned from that story elsewhere in our operation?'"

As many readers have experienced, Dan's approach is not typical. When things are tough, most people default to an approach that focuses on problems, what is not working, and who is to blame. With this focus, elephants waltz into the office and push solutions beyond reach.

Dan knew he needed to create different results, so a different operating system was needed. "Several times there was uncertainty regarding permission to discuss heated topics. I assured everyone that any topic was appropriate, with a watchful eye toward always moving forward.

"This part of the meeting lasted for well over an hour. It included some emotions that led to an esprit de corps. At the end of this portion of the meeting, I asked everyone how they felt. It was clear they felt fantastic and were on a roll!"

Dan and his team were rewarded for their efforts. When asked what role the Energy Map played in that meeting, Dan replied, "This approach helped the team identify what needed to be done. We delivered the $4 million goal—on time. Enough said."

How many million dollar meetings do you attend, where breakthroughs in thinking and results occur with such significance that they build the bottom line by up to seven figures? Such meetings are being documented around the world. The Energy Map is the guide that makes these remarkable meetings happen.

Membership in the million dollar meeting club is exclusive and open to all; you have to demonstrate your ability to guide a focus that delivers an energy, which creates a million-dollar result.

Dan Lindberg is an example of a leader who has achieved this and deliberately shaped the future. Although the challenges he and his team confront are severe, Dan has developed a culture that moves the team forward through those challenges.

By contrast, many people live at the mercy of the external circumstances of their lives, and as a result the organizations they function in do the same. Because International Truck and Engine's profits have not been where they needed to be, it would be easy to focus on all the reasons why they could not achieve their bold goals. Yet Dan's operating system—how he manages his thoughts and focus—allows him and those immediately around him to deliver a high performance when, as history proves, many leaders cannot.

What the Energy Map Is and Is Not

What the Energy Map *is not*: a strategy to avoid what is not working. What the Energy Map *is*: an authentic approach where all issues are addressed openly and honestly. What the Energy Map *is not*: a rah-rah, "focus only on the positives and ignore the smelly elephant" approach. What the Energy Map *is*: an operating system where all information is accessed and used in such a way that decisions can be made to move things forward productively.

The health of a business is determined by its employees' abilities to use the Energy Map well. This operating system allows an organization to design and sustain a focus that supports its purpose.

As you consider the Energy Map, answer these questions to build the Awareness Muscle:

- What personal and cultural operating system is being used in your organization?

- Does this operating system help people maintain a strong focus on the company's mission and values?

- Is your company's operating system aligned with its business model?

- Does your organization's operating system enhance or diminish the ability to get things done?

As the Energy Map was being introduced to his team, a leader in the quality division at a Fortune 100 company interrupted the facilitator. He had attended an earlier Wellness Culture training session and was attuned to the power of these concepts and tools. Turning to his teammates, he stated, "The key is to be aware of and control how we use our energy. How disciplined we are in the use of our energy directly correlates with how productive we are. The Energy Map may look simple, but it has greater ramifications in our lives than most of us will ever realize."

If you are like most leaders, as your Awareness Muscle grows, you will see greater opportunities to break your Leadership Lock by fine-tuning your navigating and operating system.

Decisions Determine Direction

Each of us makes thousands of decisions each day. Our focus influences our decisions, which in turn determine our direction in life.

Are you pointing your focus, and thus your energy, in the most effective direction? Charting your direction, your focus, with the Energy Map allows you to see clearly whether you are using your focus and energy to break your Leadership Lock—or tighten it. It also reveals if you are supporting—or undermining—the Wellness Culture in which you operate.

James Muir, president and CEO of Mazda Motor Europe, said, "Keeping a Forward Focus mindset and dedicating one's efforts to channeling the organization's energies in a Forward Focus manner are the qualities of leadership that I have found to deliver optimal results. Investment in explaining why something won't work or complaining about things that cannot be influenced or changed never delivers results. Keeping one's team on the front side of the Energy Map is the most powerful and rewarding experience. Once people realize this place exists, they never want to be anywhere else. In our organization, we have defied even our own expectations of success in the last three years, achieving [more than doubling] transformational revenue and profit growth.

"We have found that concentrating our energies and efforts on the front side of the Energy Map has been the catalyst for improved teamwork, accelerated and better quality execution and, above all, a healthier and happier work culture."

It is time to explore the opposing coordinates people choose from countless times a day on the Energy Map.

CHAPTER 29

The Back Side of
The Energy Map:
What Is Not Working

Focusing on What Is Not Working
Ensures More of the Same

ENERGY MAP

BACK SIDE	FRONT SIDE
WHAT'S NOT WORKING	What is working
Who/What is to blame	What we can learn
Problems	Solutions
Reasons it won't work	Objectives
	- how to get there

Because we can only focus on one thing at a time, and we go toward that focus, people who choose to focus on *what is not working* find it impossible to see *what is working*. As a result, they begin a destructive chain of events.

193

Consequences of Focusing on What Is Not Working:

- Energy and enthusiasm plummet.

- More of what is not working comes to light.

- We build a case for why we are not capable, thus inspiring hopelessness.

- Blame is assigned and people get defensive.

- Communication, creativity and productivity decline.

- Fewer risks are taken.

- Stress levels rise.

- The Humanity Factor cannot be leveraged.

Focusing on what is not working is a self-imposed handicap; people can no longer apply and leverage their intelligence, wisdom and experience. They have taken themselves out of the game.

Is It the Job or Is It You?

If you asked people to identify the aspects of their careers that are not working, undoubtedly many people could come up with a list. Some professionals carry around such an inventory daily. What do you notice about their energy and enthusiasm, their ability to live on a roll? Often, these people have little momentum in their lives. They literally cannot move forward because they are focused backward.

The Company Complainer

At some point in our careers most of us have worked with a company complainer. Their lists of things that are not working in their lives are eerily similar to company complainers we have worked with in the past. The list generally looks like this: blaming poor management, unskilled colleagues, unfair policies and a spouse who just does not understand. Then there are the complainers extraordinaire, who complain about the company complainers.

Because of the company complainer's weak Awareness Muscle, he complains no matter what company he works for. These chronic complainers use the third Mind Factor—we go toward our focus—to drive themselves, and those around them who also choose to be victims, to the back side of the Energy Map.

The 3 Mind Factors explain why we can feel poisoned in the presence of these complainers and can feel our energy draining away. If at these moments our Awareness Muscles are weak, we can unintentionally pick up the complainer's focus, thereby joining the parade to a toxic culture: wasted time, lower morale, poor job satisfaction and diminished results.

Most company complainers would not intentionally sabotage their company's progress. In many cases they are among the most loyal, hard-working employees on staff. They are simply using an old, faulty map. Their operating systems have a destructive default setting. In most cases, these people are not aware of the harm they are causing, and their Awareness Muscles are not strong enough to alert them that they have put themselves at a disadvantage.

Skilled leaders understand that these complaints are caused by the person's despair. Is it possible that people sometimes complain because of *how much they care* and because they do not have strong enough Awareness Muscles or the personal leadership skills to communicate their discontent more constructively?

"Complaining employees are actually calling for help," says the site leader for a pharmaceutical company. "As we build a stronger Wellness Culture, the complaining sticks out. How we respond to it is key."

Skilled wellness leaders understand that if they fall prey to criticizing an employee who is causing harm by complaining, they have joined this person's ranks by also focusing on *what is not working*. These leaders know that operating on the back side of the Energy Map will open the door to office elephants and doom their chances of building a Wellness Culture. They realize that desired results do not reside on the back side of the Energy Map.

CHAPTER 30

The Front Side of
The Energy Map:
What Is Working

Different Focus, Different Results

ENERGY MAP

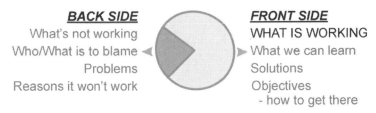

BACK SIDE	FRONT SIDE
What's not working	WHAT IS WORKING
Who/What is to blame	What we can learn
Problems	Solutions
Reasons it won't work	Objectives
	- how to get there

Focusing on *what is working* yields different results. Wellness leaders examine past experiences to mine how they created their successes and use what they learn as a foundation for building future results. This sounds easy, but most people know where minds have been trained to focus.

"When I came out of the leadership training, one of the goals I set was to reduce our backlog of orders for IV pumps," says an employee of the Heska Corporation. "By maintaining a focus on what's working rather than what's not working, we've had definite success in this area. When I first set this goal, we were looking at a six- to eight-week turnaround for orders for IV pumps. Now our turnaround is about four weeks."

 How is your team attempting to get more done—by focusing on what is not working or what IS working?

Freddy Vallejo, marketing director for O-I Ecuador, demonstrates how this application of the Energy Map creates elephant-free operations and improved results—and delivers something priceless. Freddy and his team no longer move through the day waiting to find where people are not performing or where quality is not where it should be. Instead, they make sure they spend most of their time focusing on the opposite. Freddy said, "Because we are on the front side of the Energy Map, I can tell you that we have found people we thought had no potential. Now they are becoming great assets to our company. This has made everybody way more productive."

Freddy is also one of those leaders who does not stop leading once he has left the workplace. "This approach has saved my family's future. It has changed my wife and me. We had had a destructive focus and were only seeing the bad spots in each other and our relationship. What's great is you can't see those spots when you focus on what is working. This new approach has spread to our children as well."

Freddy's embrace of the Humanity Factor and use of a new operating system at home and work has rekindled why he got into leadership in the first place. He said, "This effort is not something we have to do to earn our salaries; it's a positive approach that fulfills not only our professional goals but our personal values as well. As a result, people are more committed, more focused and happier. As directors, our jobs are way easier because trust has been established. Increasingly, we delegate important tasks to our people, and they have responded in outstanding ways. It makes me believe more than ever that people want to be great.

"Consequently, all of this has improved our output. But it's the life changes we are getting from using the Energy Map that are priceless."

Building a Can-Do Attitude in Your Team

What is a can-do attitude worth to your organization? Elephants cannot trample this much-talked-about, much-desired quality. When circumstances are difficult, when things do not seem to be moving forward, having a group of people who say, "We can do it," who are willing to fight for each other and their mutual success, is a resource few organizations enjoy.

The coveted can-do attitude does not happen by accident. This much is certain: It is not created by bringing in a motivational speaker or enticing employees with bonuses. It is not facilitated by focusing on what is not working in a department or organization. The powerful can-do attitude is created by a consistent focus on what is working. It is the attitude of "We've done it before, we can do it again—better" that gives a team access to what is possible.

"We used to harp on what was not working," said a service company leader in the Rocky Mountain region. "Looking back, this destroyed our confidence and guaranteed a weakened proficiency in our ability to overcome future obstacles. Now we are getting things done because we harp on what *is* working."

Oziel Salinas, who took his plant in Mexico from one of the poorest performing within the International Truck and Engine Corporation to the best, demonstrated his proficiency at breaking Leadership Lock. He said, "At a staff meeting, we were discussing a challenging issue. We spent half an hour discussing what failed, why, and who was to blame. Things got heated.

"Then I asked the team to stop and focus on what had worked in the past and what specific actions had been effective. Suddenly, the tone of the meeting changed. Everyone started participating and offering suggestions. In ten minutes, we solved the issue, developed an action plan and left the meeting with everyone feeling great."

Consider those moments when you were part of a group that had a strong enough Awareness Muscle to focus on what was working. How did such a practice influence the ability of individuals to move forward? Was the information collected replicated for greater successes in other parts of the organization?

Building a Can-Do Attitude for Yourself

"Before I was introduced to this approach to leadership, when I was away from work I had a tendency to focus on tasks I'd failed to accomplish at the office," one person said. "This really bugged me. But now I've started focusing on the things I *did* accomplish at work. What a difference that makes! Now, instead of agonizing over the unfinished tasks, I have the desire and energy to add them to my list of accomplishments."

Ask yourself: At the end of the day what do I focus on? Is this focus building or destroying my own can-do attitude?

Some people grow their Awareness Muscles to the point that they can see and admit their errors. Here is what an employee in the auto industry said: "Earlier in my career, I didn't fully understand the cost of being on the back side of the Energy Map, of explaining and justifying all the reasons something would be really hard to accomplish or why I might not be able to get something done. I was good at whining, and I was pretty good at making excuses up front so people didn't expect too much.

"Now I realize I was positioning myself as a victim. I wasn't just wasting my time and several other people's time, I was also developing a habitual back-side focus and an unhealthy belief system.

**"It's true that if I argue for my limitations,
I'll surely get them."**

The Elephant-Free Home:
Making Work–Life Balance Work

A president of a company listened to a group of direct reports talk about how the Energy Map was helping them bring about greater results in the workplace. As they concluded, he stood, paused and decided to raise the bar. "I'm thrilled by how we'll be moving forward at work, but let's also remember the most important work we have to do: Bring it home."

(continued on next page)

The Elephant-Free Home:
Making Work–Life Balance Work
(continued)

Each of us has come home after a tough day at work with limited time left for our families. But have you ever spent several evening hours focusing on what did not work during the day, what you did not get done, and all the problems you will face tomorrow? Did you think about the people who are making your life difficult?

"The greatest benefit of the Energy Map is that it allows us to find a work–life balance," said Rodney Montenegro of the O-I Corporation. "Every person on our team would tell you we were wasting two to three hours a day on unproductive actions driven by unproductive thoughts on the back side of the Energy Map. Not surprisingly, the moment we changed our thoughts and focus, the more effective we became at our jobs and at home. The results show that."

A focus on the back side of the Energy Map means we are carrying the worst parts of our day home with us. It means we are bringing an office elephant home so that it can give birth to a destructive little pachyderm there, too.

When we have given nearly everything we have at work, how much sense does it make to give our families and friends our leftovers?

When our families get our leftovers, the results are painful. "Things were not going well in my marriage," one training graduate wrote. "The long hours at work, the

(continued on next page)

The Elephant-Free Home:
Making Work–Life Balance Work
(continued)

kids' problems at school—everything seemed to be piling up. Any disagreement between my wife and me usually ended in a shouting match.

"Our relationship plunged. We began to talk about divorce. After being exposed to this tool, I realized I'd been using a default setting on my operating system. I knew I had to do some things differently."

The letter continues, "I started with realizing where I was on the Energy Map. As I drove home from work, I let go of my work duties and concentrated on what I was looking forward to at home. I applied the Energy Map by not ruminating on the upsets my wife and I had experienced in the past. Instead, I focused on the things my wife does well. I asked questions that were not accusatory and really listened to her responses.

"It's taken some time, but now I can communicate better with my wife, and our marriage is on the mend. Another interesting result of my change in behavior is that I can now focus better when I'm at work. Even my health is better because I'm dealing with less stress. Thank God we found a better way."

People who practice wellness leadership know that two hours at home spent focusing on what is not working is not all that is wasted. Because, as Mind Factor #3 says, we go toward what we focus on, a powerful multiplying effect kicks in: We go further in that direction. Thus, we have not only imposed two miserable hours on our family members and ourselves but, because of the

(continued on next page)

**The Elephant-Free Home:
Making Work–Life Balance Work
(continued)**

multiplying effect, we have affected the entire evening. Ultimately, this multiplying influences the next day. In some cases, it affects the rest of the week, and even a lifetime.

Top Three Results of Focusing on What Is Working

- We feel better, which is a requisite for lasting change (the first condition in the 3 Conditions That Support Change).

- Rather than allowing our successful experiences to lie dormant, we can leverage them for future progress.

- We enhance our ability to live on a roll. Elephants run from the room as higher energy and greater engagement lead to better communication and more effective problem solving. Which, not so ironically, are necessary to rectify what is not working.

CHAPTER 31

The Back Side of The Energy Map: What Is at Fault? Who Is to Blame?

How to Put the Brakes on Progress

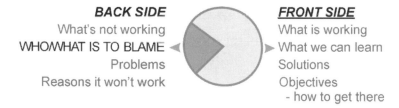

ENERGY MAP

BACK SIDE		FRONT SIDE
What's not working		What is working
WHO/WHAT IS TO BLAME		What we can learn
Problems		Solutions
Reasons it won't work		Objectives
		- how to get there

Not surprisingly, the elements of the back side of the Energy Map weigh us down in a number of destructive ways. When a team focuses on what is not working, the hunt for fault and blame begins.

The B-Lame Game

Despite their size, elephants do not always come crashing through the front door. They can be subtle. Particularly when the B-Lame Game is played. Teams engaged in this contest render their organizations lame. The elephants they spawn seep through cubicles, creep under office doors and stain boardroom floors and walls. Never mind the competition; companies afflicted with this ailment self-destruct.

If we blame, we will be lame.

Some leaders construct cultures that prey on mistakes. Status and careers are built on the premise of leading error-free operations. Make a mistake and you are castigated. Perhaps a personal agenda has been impeded, or the error may reveal an area in which the leader is not skilled. We all know people made of such cloth. They believe that, for them to succeed, two things must happen:

1. They must not fail. Therefore, mistakes—their own and those of the people who work for them—cannot be tolerated.

2. Those around them must fail. Their flawed logic reasons that if others fail, then they will succeed.

Those who work in organizations that consistently deliver excellent results have learned that mistakes are unavoidable. Mistakes do not inherently slow a company down. It is the response to mistakes that often proves to be a burden.

How to Perpetuate Mistakes

In a work culture where the B-Lame Game is the norm, the elephant shows up as employees who are uncomfortable and fearful. People are so busy pointing fingers and, as the popular saying goes, engaging in "CYA" activities that there are no hands left to do the work. They are reluctant to offer ideas or respond to requests to think out of the box or take greater ownership. These symptoms indicate an illness—an illness that stems in part from employees' experiences with past mistakes. When mistakes were made, hands were not just slapped; human dignity was crushed. Ironically, more mistakes occur in these environments because people do not feel good about themselves or their employers.

The burden of unproductive time caused by the weight of blame is staggering. Hours are lost not just in the wake of mistakes but because the company's strength is whittled away before the next task or project begins.

Here are results of the B-Lame Game. Do you recognize any of these signs?

- Defensiveness

- Disengagement

- Turf protection

- Employee turnover

- Broken trust

- Stifled creativity

- Reduced risk taking

- Low accountability

- An overfed office elephant

A team with the need to lay blame or make excuses is like a person with pneumonia running a marathon. The debilitated cannot compete.

A Sure Way to Make
Yourself Powerless at Work

"Did you see the new form the finance department is making us fill out?" John asked.

"Who hasn't?" replied Grace. "As if we don't have enough paperwork."

John threw a dart at his dartboard. "They're clueless over there."

"Well, I can tell you I'm not going to make my numbers," Grace said. "When Fred wants to know why, I'll just hand him my file of finance forms. But he probably won't get the point."

"Hey, he's as clueless as they are," John replied, releasing another dart.

Have you ever overheard an exchange like this? People who have conversations of this sort create Leadership Lock for themselves and others.

It is no mystery why people who use this operating system deliver marginal results. Because they can only focus on one thing at a time, they cannot engage in a B-Lame Game conversation and be on the front side of the Energy Map at the same time. Because they consistently focus on who or what is to blame, they cannot focus on what they might learn. They do not see how they could generate different results. They are not aware of what options they have or how they can contribute.

These people are victims of the external circumstances of their lives. In a world where those who can lead themselves effectively hold power, they have taken themselves out of the race. They have become powerless. They are left with nothing to do but throw darts.

When events in your life seem bigger than you, what do you do to take responsibility? How do you use such Magic Moments? Do you consistently exercise your Awareness Muscle so you are conscious of your ability to choose to be a victim or to take responsibility?

Top Three Implications of Focusing on Blame

- We cannot move forward.

- We adopt the role of victim.

- *We* become part of the problem.

CHAPTER 32

The Front Side of The Energy Map: What We Can Learn

Moving from "Trial and Error"
to "Trial and Learn"

ENERGY MAP

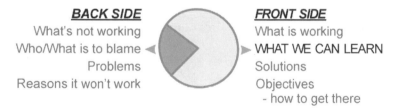

BACK SIDE
What's not working
Who/What is to blame
Problems
Reasons it won't work

FRONT SIDE
What is working
WHAT WE CAN LEARN
Solutions
Objectives
- how to get there

What is required for a leader to shift a culture from the attitude of *who or what is to blame* to *what we can learn*? From a trial-and-error approach to an operating system of trial and learn? Wellness leaders know the answer is as simple as what types of questions they ask and what people focus on.

211

A participant in a training session held in Japan said, "It's only a mistake if we don't learn from it. And we're not going to learn from it if we're busy blaming each other."

The Resource Generator

"We don't have the resources." This is a frequent, disappointing phrase that is not always accurate. What would be the value to your organization if you could actually create additional resources without increasing expenditures?

Sound impossible? Some leaders reading this book are chuckling because they know this *is* possible. They realize that many of their competitors, in an effort to eliminate waste, have turned their backs on the ingredients necessary for developing additional resources. The ingredients: mistakes and wellness leadership.

When mistakes occur, wellness leaders are in their finest form. They know that, more than leading people, they are leading focus. So these leaders quickly convert mistakes into resources. Because of the never-ending demand for additional resources, for methods to increase profit margins, talented leaders *generate* resources through their actions.

The #1 Fuel for Resource Generators: Mistakes

Rather than loathing errors or putting elephants on the backs of their teams with a focus of blame or fear, leaders who are resource generators use a healthy operating system. They use the front side of the Energy Map to turn mistakes or obstacles into resources.

Questions for Transforming Mistakes into Resources

- What steps can we take to regain peak efficiency?

- What approaches have worked well for us in the past?

- What could we have done differently that we will want to use as a lesson in the future?

- What have we discovered about the team and ourselves that makes us stronger?

- Is there a personnel decision that would better serve an individual, the team and the organization?

- As we move forward, how will we know we are on track? How will we measure our progress in this area?

"Business has been extremely intense lately," said Axel Schunck of Mazda Motor Europe. "There is so little time to get everything done. We understand that any time we invest in looking for who is guilty means that our chances of finding solutions dwindle away. I'm most proud of our team because we spend almost all our time looking for things we can learn and for solutions to the issues facing us. The results we're getting prove that this focus is making a difference."

Mistakes, or an undesired outcome, do not have a preordained routing system on any person's Energy Map. They are not bad or good; the person dealing with the outcome decides that. This person decides if events and time will be squandered or leveraged.

Converting mistakes into resources is not about creating a culture that encourages mistakes. It is not about being consequence-free when mistakes happen or allowing people to skirt responsibility. It is not about being weak and condoning poor quality or bad behavior.

It is about leading with a focus that frees the organization to execute strategies effectively and without restraint.

It is about developing people and relationships upstream to ensure that exceptional quality and outstanding behaviors are the norm downstream. It is about supporting the thinkers and leaders around us. It is about being forward focused.

How will you quickly and effectively use the mistakes you and others make today to achieve better results tomorrow? How can you use these same mistakes to develop greater trust and relationships?

Leadership's Greatest Frontier

Operating on the front side of the Energy Map is not easy. Focusing on what is working and what we can learn, particularly when things are difficult, is not common. Could it be that making this shift represents a significant upgrade in leadership?

Intelligence, skill proficiency and the ability to deliver results are often considered the jewels, or must-haves, of leadership. Is it possible that an organization sells itself short if its mantra is "it's all about results"? What happens if every organization is screaming for greater results—what then separates one organization from another?

The answer obviously lies in *how* those results are delivered.

Our interviews reveal that most people in business attempt to deliver results by playing with spreadsheets, making demands, telling others what to do, relying on external motivation, hoping and using the threat of consequences, among other strategies. These age-old tactics, and the toxic culture they generate, get handed down from one generation to another. So do the average results they deliver.

Yet business is evolving at lightning speed. In addition, technology has advanced so much that it has to wait for us. And communication? The speed of communication is allowing us to do more than ever imagined.

But what has not evolved? What is literally holding the whole world back? Leadership. *How* we lead others and ourselves.

That is about to change. Leadership is on the verge of leaving the Dark Ages, and every one of us has the ability to help make that happen. No longer does the command-and-control or carrot-and-stick style of leadership cut it. No longer does insulting others by telling them what to do get us where we need to go.

People are tired of this approach. In fact, they are becoming immune to it. They are sick of leaders who worry only about themselves and the bottom line. They want more. They want leaders who think holistically, who think about the workplace culture, who think about families. They want leaders who involve them, acknowledge them, guide them, inspire them and deliver more for them.

Such leaders are wanted not just in business but in our communities and in our government. They are wanted—needed—in our homes.

Here is a key to perhaps the largest Leadership Lock of all: We will not see this evolution in leadership by judging those who use outdated leadership tactics. Because of the Mind Factor that says *we go toward our focus,* our criticism and flaw-assessment of such people will only secure a future much like today.

Instead, this great change in leadership is an action item on each of our agendas, regardless of our position or title. It begins with our thinking and is grounded in the mission to build others up rather than control them. It depends on our ability to assess *our* responses and how *our* actions affect others and ourselves.

We are not alone in this endeavor. There are many others out there like you—people who want and are delivering stellar results *and* who know that, at the end of the day and at the end of their careers, equally important is the positive difference they have made.

**It all comes down to this: focus and energy.
The more skilled we are at controlling our own,
the more apt we are to successfully guide
focus and energy in others.**

CHAPTER 33

The Back Side Of the Energy Map: Problems

No Rose-Colored Glasses Allowed

ENERGY MAP

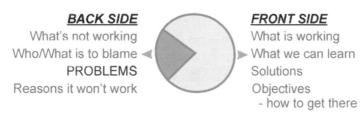

BACK SIDE
What's not working
Who/What is to blame
PROBLEMS
Reasons it won't work

FRONT SIDE
What is working
What we can learn
Solutions
Objectives
- how to get there

Is the Energy Map about ignoring or avoiding problems? Is it a blindly optimistic approach reserved for those wearing rose-colored glasses?

When we ask these questions in trainings, participants consistently shake their heads no. Problems must be resolved if individuals and organizations are to achieve success. Ineffectual leaders who avoid tough issues sap the energy and resources needed to move forward.

217

Ironically, if we try to ignore or avoid our problems, or analyze our problems, what is our focus? *Problems*—a denizen of the back side of the Energy Map. Because we go toward our focus, we are guaranteed to find even more problems. No leader wants to create more problems for himself or his organization, yet without this awareness, leaders often sabotage their own intentions and efforts.

**Enlightened leaders know that problems
do not happen. Rather, events happen,
and because of a destructive focus,
the events are distinguished as problems.
Results are instantly jeopardized.**

When a team of engineers was introduced to this element of the back side of the Energy Map, in unison they all put their pens down, leaned back and crossed their arms in mute resistance—except for one. He understood. "I get it," he said. "It's our job to *understand* the problem, so we know what the issue is, so we can find a solution. If we continue to focus on the problem, it's impossible to discover a solution."

**Somehow, many of us were conditioned
to believe that, to get ahead, we are
supposed to look behind. Is it possible
that the traditional method of dealing with
problems is what causes problems
for organizations in the first place?**

Elephant Meetings

The next time you are in a meeting, pay attention to the response from others when someone launches a statement with, "The problem is . . ." Observe what happens to people's posture, their energy and creativity, and the productivity of the meeting. If you get a chance, notice what happens to the effectiveness of the people who participated in the meeting after they return to their desks.

All of us have heard choruses of toxic opinions describing the endless problems associated with a particular person, subject or project.

Every minute a team focuses on problems is a minute it cannot focus on solutions.

Money slips away as colleagues propel themselves and others further from results, which are found only on the front side of the Energy Map. Attitudes, forever a by-product of focus, are pulled down like a fishing bobber with a fish on the line—and a smelly fish at that.

Numerous leaders we have partnered with have stated, "In our effort to reduce waste, we have finally discovered the source of our greatest waste: time spent on the back side of the Energy Map."

You Make the Call

Which statement or question do you prefer?

- "The problem with your work is . . ." or "What we must see more of is . . ."

- "Our problem is that we . . ." or "What we must improve on is . . ."

- "What is the problem?" or "What is the issue you want to address?"

If you chose the latter statements and questions, you chose a form of communication that is direct, honest and focuses on solutions, a front-side-of-the-Energy-Map approach that produces greater results more efficiently.

Many organizations approach us asking how to improve communication, develop problem-solving skills and enhance team identity. Is it possible those organizations have not sufficiently developed these attributes because people have been using words that keep teams meandering on the back side of the Energy Map? If so, how will changing the focus, and thus the words, affect a team in these critical areas?

Educated as an engineer, Carol Story of International Truck and Engine Corporation was quite familiar and admittedly comfortable with problem analysis. But she found herself in positions in which being analytical did not get the needed response. "I never would have imagined there was another way to approach challenges," she said. "To think that my focus and choice of words have the effect on others that they do has had a profound impact on my ability to lead effectively."

Results of Focusing on Problems

- Problems become bigger. We major in problems because we study them all day.

- Because we go toward our focus, we will always find more problems. How many problems are enough?

- Teamwork deteriorates. Because problems usually mean someone did something wrong, focusing on them breeds defensiveness, reduced quality and a culture of blame.

- We impede our own progress. Focusing on problems creates obstacles that have to be overcome later if we are to move forward. A focus on problems is a death sentence to initiatives for change.

- Resources vanish. When a team invests in studying the problem, how much time and money are left for focusing on solutions?

- The fix-it approach is perpetuated. Traditional, back-side thinking says that by studying problems a team ensures that problems will not recur. But with this approach, energy, teamwork and creativity—all of which are required for finding solutions and moving forward—are trampled by an entire herd of elephants.

The Back-Side-of-the-Energy-Map Guarantee

Focusing on problems, or any other aspect of the back side of the Energy Map, gives an organization a number of guarantees, including disengaged employees. When a company uses an operating system that focuses on problems, it systematically slays the desire of employees to be great, leaving them disillusioned and disengaged.

Consider the disengaged employees in your organization. What if the reason they are disengaged is because of their focus, a focus given to them by the culture in which they are immersed? In a short amount of time, a person with a more constructive focus can begin to turn this tide.

CHAPTER 34

Events Are Waiting To Be Labeled— By You

Issues Are in the Middle of the Energy Map—
Waiting for Backward or Forward Energy

ENERGY MAP

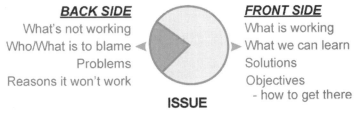

BACK SIDE	FRONT SIDE
What's not working	What is working
Who/What is to blame	What we can learn
Problems	Solutions
Reasons it won't work	Objectives - how to get there

ISSUE

Shakespeare said, "There is nothing either good or bad but thinking makes it so." Stuff happens. Events and issues occur. Challenges come up continually; they are a permanent part of doing business, of living. When something happens, each one of us determines whether we make it difficult or easy for people

223

around us to handle those events; each one of us determines in which direction on the Energy Map we take the issues.

Think about the leaders who have made the greatest difference in your life. Undoubtedly they have many things in common, such as the following:

- They choose to position outcomes not as problems but as issues or challenges, and in some cases, even as opportunities.

- They understand that life is made up of issues, one after another, and that there is a solution for each one.

- They know there is no finish line. They see every issue and how it fits into the long-term picture, therefore leveraging every moment.

- These leaders bring out the best in us, because they lead us to the front side of the Energy Map. They often create an excitement around the work being done.

Energy, or power, is transferred when problems are reframed as *issues*. Issues—contract negotiations, work of poor quality, a disengaged employee, an unethical friend, marital conflicts—lie at the center of the Energy Map waiting to see which side the leader will take them to. "Being on the front side of the Energy Map doesn't mean that issues—formerly known as problems—don't come up," said Michelle McKim, marketing coordinator at the Heska Corporation. "It means we're able to tackle them more efficiently and effectively."

Some special leaders are masterful at directing focus and using all events as resources. Dan Morris, director and senior managing executive officer in charge of marketing, sales and customer service for Mazda Motor Corporation, comprehends with absolute clarity that the tough times—the challenges, the *issues*—are the Magic Moments for his organization.

Before holding his current position, Dan was president and CEO of Mazda Motor Europe. During his time at the helm, the organization moved from the least profitable division within Mazda to the top. The division made this jump by posting the largest increase in sales while keeping costs low. "The Wellness Culture approach solidified our management team into a cohesive, high-performing working group and energized us to accomplish even greater results," said Dan. Mazda Motor Europe is "achieving results more quickly, and our issues and challenges are much easier to overcome. Bottom line: The front-side-of-the-Energy-Map approach works."

Not coincidentally, Dan's achievements were recognized within the Ford-Mazda system worldwide. He was rewarded with a seat on Mazda's board of directors and a promotion to lead Mazda's global marketing, sales and customer service team. He attributes this achievement to his diligence in functioning from the front side of the Energy Map.

Twists and Turns of the Weather Vane

Issues are opportunities for leaders to make their most significant impacts on the direction of a company. An unskilled leader, unaware of the consequences of operating on the back side of the Energy Map, will twist and turn like a weather vane in a wind storm, looking for the latest remedy, the quickest fix, the easy way out. A skilled leader operates like a river; he sees the issue and, knowing the power and reward of forward focus, moves his team toward its objective. The river may have to flow through rapids, it may be dammed, but it will not be denied.

Top Three Implications of
Positioning Problems as Issues:

1. Our perspective is our reality. Why not choose a perspective that creates a reality conducive to results?

2. People want to be around you.

3. Individuals and organizations are free to move forward.

CHAPTER 35

The Front Side Of the Energy Map: Solutions

Focus on Solutions and More Will Appear

ENERGY MAP

BACK SIDE
What's not working
Who/What is to blame
Problems
Reasons it won't work

FRONT SIDE
What is working
What we can learn
SOLUTIONS
Objectives
- how to get there

ISSUES

Just as focusing on problems begets more problems, the reverse is true for those who seek solutions. Focusing on solutions generates more than just solutions; it yields positive by-products as well.

Side Effects of Focusing on Solutions:

- Greater confidence

- Stronger proficiencies in executing strategies

- Enhanced creativity

- More willingness to collaborate

- Improved self-esteem

- Increased likelihood of realizing potential

- Ready access to the lessons of past experience

- Excitement builds and more work gets done

Unlike those who use outdated maps, which trap people in destructive operating systems and prevent them from moving forward, leaders who focus on solutions can *only move forward.* They see only solutions because that is what they focus on.

A state governor and his staff received complaints that it was taking too long to process applications for food assistance. In an effort to resolve the issue, the governor went directly to the manager in charge, explained the problem, and asked him to take care of it.

The manager assembled his team and asked, "Why is it taking so long to process these applications?" Not surprisingly, this focus on the back side of the Energy Map exacerbated the problem. Energy was expended in finger pointing, sharing excuses and acting defensively, yielding little forward progress.

After some coaching, the manager approached the team again—except this time he asked a different question: "What can we do to process these applications more quickly?" Predictably, this question elicited different responses. These responses cut the application time in half.

What issue is your team currently facing as a problem? In what area do you feel it is time to let go of the burden of problems and begin focusing on solutions?

Questions Aimed at Focusing on Solutions:

- What specifically am I focused on now—analyzing problems or exploring solutions?

- What is the cost of focusing on the back side of the Energy Map? What is the cost to my energy? Enthusiasm? Creativity? Ability to be on a roll?

- What are some of the greatest benefits for me and those around me as I shift to a focus on solutions?

- What approaches that have worked well in the past might assist me now?

- What do I ultimately want to accomplish?

- Why is this objective important?

- What ideas will move us closer to our objective?

What advantages would you give yourself, your colleagues, company and family if, when facing a challenge, you immediately saw opportunity?

Justin Scheuchenzuber, vice president of field operations at Navistar Financial Corporation (NFC), said that "one office was behind in processing entries, and this had a potentially significant impact on results for NFC." By accepting the reality of the situation and taking the responsibility of the High Road, as Justin said, he and his team "focused on what was working, solutions and what we could learn." The results were quick and impressive: a 50 percent improvement in one month. "Now we're working upstream on a process that will prevent this from happening again."

How Solutions Come to Us

Focusing on solutions does not mean we get to show up at work and find the answers we need wrapped in a pretty package tied with a bow. Like baking cookies with a four-year-old, finding solutions can be a messy task. But messy does not have to mean harmful.

A Case Study: The Messy Meeting

Jackson threw down the analysis, stood up and went for it. "I know you've got your reasons, but this just doesn't make sense to me. All the indicators point to the Southeast region. *All* of them!" His hands were raised as if he were holding the world above his head. His voice cracked, but he pushed on. "Every outlet in the Southeast is kicking butt!" He looked squarely at the man at the end of the table, who happened to be the company's president. "Now is not the time to experiment in the West region!"

The president stared back at Jackson, leaving his arms folded on his chest. Before he could say anything, Becky, sitting next to him, extended her hands, as if to invite Jackson her way. She said, "But don't you see? It's the success in the Southeast that will allow us to test new markets!"

She looked at the president, then continued. "Jackson, we wouldn't be in the Southeast if it wasn't for our success in the *Northe*ast region. Can't you see how it's the logical next step?"

Betty, Kristin and Joel all jumped into the fray. They spoke simultaneously, until Kristin raised her voice and prevailed. "I'd be in favor of expansion, but we must see the numbers to support it." Now that she had control of the table, Kristin made eye contact with the other members of the team. "Jackson, I don't know where you're getting your butt-kicking numbers. Seeing those is a must. Becky, we haven't seen solid evidence that the West region will bite. And pardon me, but I believe we must figure out why we were successful in the Northeast before we go anywhere!"

The room fell quiet. Apparently, after an intense two hours, everyone had said his or her piece. They looked at the president as he put his elbows on the table and smiled.

"An observation." He waited for a moment. "I sense exhaustion rather than tension. Passion rather than anger. And commitment rather than compliance."

He stood up and put his hands in his pockets. "I'm proud of us. We started this meeting by dedicating ourselves to a course that sought solutions. We agreed we would spend no time focusing on problems, whether those problems were in someone's proposal, someone's attitude or someone's ideas." He smiled. "And you followed through. As a result, we got to hear *everyone's* ideas, *everyone's* thoughts. And that, my friends, is important." He took his hands out of his pockets to clasp them in front of him. "It's important because this healthy debate is vital for our success. How we operate, how we control our focus, will be the defining advantage we have over our competitors."

Becky looked up at the man standing next to her. "But we didn't resolve anything, Jerry. We didn't make any decisions."

"And gratefully so, Becky," he replied. "If we had made a decision at any point before now, it would have been premature and thus riddled with risks." He smiled. "The decision must and will come soon. What excites me most is that with continued, passionate debate, we'll unearth a solution we can't even conceptualize right now."

Jackson spoke up. "What are you talking about, Jerry?"

"I'm talking about solutions. *Real,* step-level solutions don't necessarily present themselves in a two-hour meeting. In addition, the solutions we seek will hide from us if we focus on our problems and what hasn't worked in the past. That's why I'm so proud of this team—you stayed forward focused." He paused. "And you don't need me to remind you that we all want the same thing: success for the organization. Because you know this, you have brought to the table a high level of respect for each other."

He sipped from his glass of water, then continued. "This combination of factors is allowing us to dig deep and find the solutions that will enable us to reach our goal—to be number one." He smiled at the entire team. "It's not easy, but that doesn't mean it can't be fun."

The silence that filled the room spoke for everyone on the team. Their leader was right. Though they hadn't reached a decision, they had made significant progress as they collectively gained new information and a new perspective. They sensed a building energy in the room that meant something dear to them: a conviction that breakthrough results were on the horizon.

Phil broke the silence. "Who's hungry?"

"I am. And you're buyin'," Jackson said, as he threw a wadded piece of paper at his colleague.

"I'm buying?" Phil responded. "Oh, no. Not me."
He threw the paper at Becky. "It's her turn."

The room erupted into a new debate. The president smiled. *Right on course.*

The Advantages of Forward Focus

Bottom line: Your organization's success depends on its ability to generate solutions. Employing talented people is only part of the equation; talent and skill will get you only so far. Equally important is effectively coordinating that talent; aligning people with purpose delivers profitability.

Wellness leaders know that as they develop a Wellness Culture, they can make better use of one of the prime levers for capitalizing on talent: vigorous debate. Conducted in a healthy manner, debate provides an exponential return on the skill and wisdom within the room, unlocking solutions necessary for the life of the company.

If vigorous debate

1. focuses on solutions,

2. builds on what has worked in the past and the lessons of what has not worked in the past, and

3. is framed with the understanding that everyone wants to be great and wants the organization to succeed,

it permits

1. increased participation (because people do not waste time getting defensive),

2. expanded ideas (because thoughts are augmented instead of cut down),

3. maximization of the talent and experience available (because an environment of full engagement is fostered),

which results in

1. the discovery of more effective solutions, which fosters

2. a stronger team identity that includes trust and confidence, which generates

3. ownership, alignment and execution of action plans, which delivers

4. greater business results.

Vigorous debate is vital because it allows full truth telling and information flow. Without it, a herd of elephants roams the corridors, severely limiting the success of strategies.

> **Building a stronger Wellness Culture allows your team to discuss and debate the brutal truth rather than addressing the truth brutally.**

One participant in a session approached us afterwards and said, "Everyone keeps telling us how important vigorous debate is, but before now no one has ever told us what stops it and what allows it to happen. The Energy Map explains it all."

Vigorous debate happens when people move their focus to the front side of the Energy Map.

CHAPTER 36

The Back Side Of the Energy Map: All the Reasons It Won't Work

Strategy-Eating Elephants Love This Focus

ENERGY MAP

BACK SIDE
What's not working
Who/What is to blame
Problems
REASONS IT WON'T WORK

ISSUES

FRONT SIDE
What is working
What we can learn
Solutions
Objectives
 - how to get there

All the great innovations, the breakthroughs in any industry—
Ford's assembly line, Dell's customized PCs, Apple's iPod—
started as ideas. From conception to reality, those ideas may
have taken a beating, but eventually they evolved into seminal
events. But they did not get their opportunity for glory in the
marketplace on their own. Ideas need leaders.

Sometimes people take themselves, their teams and their families out of the contest before an idea gets to the starting line. How? Even before the starting gun goes off, they focus on all the reasons why an idea or strategy will not work.

- What happens around you when ideas are volunteered?

- What happens to creative conversations when people focus on all the reasons why something will not work?

- What happens to emotions as a person sees his ideas punctured without even being considered?

- As a result, what happens to the prospects for synergy and the potential for future ideas?

The back side of the Energy Map can appear to be a safe place; users of this "excuses" approach often focus on why an idea will not work to defend themselves from risks, from the unknown. Focusing on the reasons why something *might* work frequently means things will change. For some people, this is a hazard to be avoided. It means they might have to work, to put forth a refined effort. Therefore, when a new idea comes along, they move to discredit or sabotage it by focusing on the reasons why it will not work.

Tim Foley, of International Truck and Engine Corporation, has helped numerous people become more effective leaders by managing focus and energy. "The back side of the Energy Map is the known side. It holds nothing new. It's all data we've collected. Therefore, it can seem safe," said Tim. "The front side of the Energy Map is the unknown. It's where possibility lies. That can seem pretty scary for some. But it's where you have to go if you want to move forward."

Reasons Why a Person Might Focus
on Why an Idea Won't Work:

- "It wasn't my idea."

- "I am afraid of failing."

- "I'm afraid my efforts will not be perfect."

- "I'm worried about losing control, power or status."

- "It's not the way we do things around here."

- "I'm not going to do it because I was not involved in the decision."

- "It didn't work when we tried it last time."

- "We don't have enough resources for anything different."

None of us can justify pointing a finger at someone who carries the "why it won't work" shield because all of us have used such excuses at one time or another.

Is it possible that, when things are not moving forward as we hoped, it is not because of the idea but because of our response to the idea?

*Top Implications of Focusing
on Why Something Will Not Work:*

- If the only strategies that work are those we are doing now, improvement is impossible.

- We block our own potential and limit our ability to be excited about work.

- We can count on being excluded from future brainstorming sessions.

The Most Important Audit in Your Organization and Family

The most important audit an organization or family conducts is the idea audit. It is an analysis that occurs the moment someone offers a new idea.

Destructive Questions in the Typical Idea Audit:

- "Is it a good idea or a bad one?"

- "What is the effect of this idea on my idea?"

- "Whose idea was this?"

- "What will be required of my staff and me if we use this idea?"

- "How much will the idea cost me or us?"

Ideas are like oxygen to an organization. Without new ideas, a company asphyxiates itself. Companies that do not generate new ideas are not beaten by the competition; they beat themselves.

 How well does your organization conduct an idea audit?

A Case Study: The Idea Audit, Part I

The idea struck John while he was sitting at a traffic light, of all places. Just like that—*blink*—the idea was there. He had not put together the details, but his heart raced as he headed to the executive meeting. He had been invited to offer some ideas, and he grinned as he imagined his supervisor's response.

Once the meeting started, the president muttered a few statements about declining revenue, and the twenty-two people around the table fell silent. Eventually, the marketing VP leaned forward and offered an idea. "We could realign our branding efforts by moving away from a singular, business-unit perspective and moving toward an overall image."

"What?" the VP of finance asked. "Do you have any idea what that would cost? Besides, we just invested a ton two years ago on expanding product identity."

"And given the restructuring that's already taken place, everyone's on pins and needles," the HR rep offered. "I don't think we can support anything that hints of realignment."

The room grew quiet again. John looked at the president, then at his supervisor. He decided to go for it and cleared his dry throat. "I was sitting at a red light on First Avenue when this idea struck me," he chuckled. When the response was limited to blank stares, he quickly continued. "We're spending a lot of resources on coordinating efforts between our Denver facility and the Chicago plant. I'm wondering what we could do to reduce costs, improve quality and increase productivity if we took a close look at the processes involved with that."

The VP of production nearly choked on the cookie he was chewing. "Are you proposing we move production to Denver?"

"Well, not necessarily, but I'm wondering—"

Production cut him off. "That ain't gonna happen on my watch! We've streamlined our efforts and are cutting on a dime. Don't give me some cockeyed idea about moving."

John sat back in his seat, realizing he hadn't introduced his idea well enough. He tried again. "I'm not suggesting we move anybody. But from my perspective, the coordination between the two locations could improve."

"Could improve?" the VP of information technology said, with his eyebrows pressing more tightly together. "What are you talking about?"

"Well," John said, shrugging his shoulders. "If the folks at the two sites knew each other better and understood each other's objectives . . ." He hesitated. ". . . maybe they could execute better."

"That's not going to make any difference," HR spoke up again. "We've been sending the sites through teamwork exercises together for years. We've got it covered."

"The problem with your idea is that you think execution is the problem." It was the Denver general manager's turn. "We've got no problems with execution."

That wasn't the data John had. He tried to clarify. "But . . ."

His supervisor, who leaned over and patted him on the shoulder, cut him off. "Thanks, John. Don't take it personally. But I recommend you don't hit red lights on your way to work." Everyone laughed, grateful for the break in tension.

The room returned to silence. Finally, the president spoke up. "Okay," he drew a deep breath. "Looks like we'll be back here again tomorrow—and the next day, until someone has an idea that will work."

The Idea Audit, Part II

The idea struck Jim while he was sitting at a traffic light, of all places. Just like that—*blink*—the idea was there. He had not put together the details, but his heart raced as he headed to the executive meeting. He had been invited to offer some ideas, and he grinned as he imagined his supervisor's response.

Once the meeting started, the president shared his concern about declining revenues and stated how critical it was that fresh ideas be generated. The twenty-two people sitting around the table jumped to life. The marketing VP had the loudest voice and prevailed. "We could realign our branding efforts by moving away from a singular, business-unit perspective and moving toward an overall image."

Everyone sat quietly for a moment as they considered this. Then the VP of finance spoke up. "I like the idea of enhancing our overall brand image. That would never hurt." His fingers danced silently on the table. "Any ideas on what the logistics and costs would look like for such a move?"

The marketing VP shook his head. "Not off the top of my head, but I could get some numbers to you in a week."

"Could we do that together?" HR interjected. "We've gone through a lot of restructuring lately. I think everyone's on pins and needles, so I want to make sure a move like this would consider the impact on personnel as it evolves."

"No sweat," Marketing responded. "Let's do it on Thursday after our meeting on payroll."

Jim saw his chance and cleared his throat. "I was sitting at a red light on First Avenue when this idea struck me," he chuckled. When the response was limited to blank stares, he quickly continued. "We're spending a lot of resources on coordinating efforts between our Denver facility and the Chicago plant. I'm wondering what we could do to reduce costs, improve quality and increase productivity if we took a close look at the processes involved with that."

The VP of production nearly choked on the cookie he was chewing. "Are you proposing we move production to Denver?"

"Well, not necessarily, but I'm wondering . . ."

"I don't think anything's being proposed yet," Jim's supervisor interrupted. "What we're looking for are ideas."

The production VP took another bite of his cookie and slumped back in his seat.

Suddenly Purchasing leaned forward. "I've never thought about this until now, but maybe from our end we could coordinate the purchasing efforts. That would require buy-in and ownership from both facilities, but it might be worth looking at."

Jim had not thought about the purchasing perspective but nodded because he liked the momentum. Then he said, "Coordinating efforts between the two locations could improve."

"Could improve?" the IT VP said, with his eyebrows pressing more tightly together. "What are you talking about?"

"Well," Jim said, shrugging his shoulders. "If the folks at the two sites knew each other better and understood each other's objectives . . ." He paused. ". . . maybe they could execute better."

"We've been sending the sites through leadership exercises together for years," HR spoke up. "Do you think there's a way to have a greater impact?"

"I'm not sure," Jim said. "I haven't thought this through yet. All I know is the numbers aren't adding up between the two sites."

"What I like about your idea, Jim, is that it speaks to execution." It was the Denver general manager's turn. "Anytime we can achieve better execution, I'm all ears."

"So am I," the president said as he stood up. "Jim might be on to something. Let's do a small group breakout. Take twenty minutes to take a close look at your responsibilities between Denver and Chicago. When we come back, we'll put all the possibilities on the table and see where this idea goes."

As they got up from their seats, Jim's supervisor leaned over, patted him on the shoulder, and said loud enough for everyone to hear, "I recommend you hit more red lights on your way to work." Everyone laughed.

How Do We Deal with Bad Ideas?

Every organization has ideas. Because people want to be great, ideas are a natural outgrowth of a Wellness Culture. But the challenge lies not only in generating ideas.

Equally important is an organization's ability to create an environment that nurtures and develops ideas once they are offered. This ability provides companies with a strategic advantage that separates them from their competitors.

Realistically, however, if some ideas were implemented, the results could cost an organization or a family vital resources and a healthy culture. Given that, how do we point out potential roadblocks without dampening energy and spirits, stalling momentum and limiting change? How do we respond if an idea stinks?

The answer: We stay on the front side of the Energy Map. We tell the truth by clearly stating our perspective as it relates to the *objective*. We examine the idea's potential from the perspective of how it might work as it relates to the objectives that must be achieved. If indeed the idea will not be as effective as other ideas, this exploration process will uncover the fact that it should be modified or abandoned in favor of a better idea.

Productive Questions for a Successful Idea Audit:

- "What elements of the idea could help us?"

- "How does this idea move us further toward our objective?"

- "How can we now improve on this idea?"

- "What other ideas do we want to consider?"

- "If we implement this idea, what would be the wisest use of our resources right now?"

- "What role can I or our team play to best develop or implement this idea?"

CHAPTER 37

The Front Side Of the Energy Map: The Objective and How to Get There

Focusing on the Objective Creates Synergies
and Gets Us Where We Need to Go

ENERGY MAP

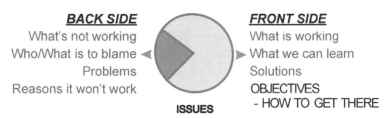

BACK SIDE
What's not working
Who/What is to blame
Problems
Reasons it won't work

ISSUES

FRONT SIDE
What is working
What we can learn
Solutions
OBJECTIVES
- HOW TO GET THERE

People who successfully use the 3 Mind Factors to navigate through the events of a day spend no time considering why something will not work; instead, they are relentless in pointing at the objective and exploring how to get there. Energy is everything to these people. They build a Wellness Culture around them and function on a roll, knowing that these two requisites will create the conditions for breakthrough results.

Do you know people and teams that are in so much Leadership Lock that they rarely recognize their objectives? Such groups have a distinguishing characteristic: They sacrifice progress in exchange for the mythical "perfect idea or solution." From your experience, how often does a perfect solution appear?

In other words, most ideas and strategies are met by a choir singing the "why it won't work" theme song because flaws are identified and studied. This is the opposite of creating synergies by trying ideas, learning from them, building on them and moving toward the objective.

Once again, focus and energy either ride to the rescue in finding the solution to get to the goal, or they drag everyone and everything back to the starting line.

The Cost of a "Results Only" Focus

Wall Street has made the tactic of focusing on results a popular practice. As stated earlier, "Results Driven" is a mantra that is quickly becoming trite—as is the leadership approach that accompanies it.

No one here is suggesting that results are not important. They are vital. Ironically, some leaders rob their teams of needed energy by focusing only on outcomes. This means their teams can only be reactive and take a fix-it approach. Outcomes, goals and objectives, of course, are the variables of effect. While objectives are essential, they are not achieved by telling, demanding or bribing others to perform. Because goals are outcomes, wellness leaders go upstream and focus on the variables of cause.

The most influential cause of results within any organization is how people function together.

A wellness leader uses the Energy Map as a filter for his thoughts. It can help him determine if he is using a map with outdated information and approaches or if he is processing healthy, productive information and using approaches and words that move everyone toward their goals.

This leader uses the front side of the Energy Map to ensure that the only person who can stop them—himself—does not. He keeps the objective firmly in mind and continually refines how to get there.

A manufacturing company in Thailand put this concept to work. While negotiating terms with two suppliers, members of the company's leadership team were tempted to focus on the fact that what was being proposed was unacceptable. This, of course, was the equivalent of focusing on the back side of the Energy Map, with all the reasons it would not work. Although this approach is often the standard in negotiations, it frequently results in lengthy delays, bitter relationships and poor quality.

A leader named Met and his colleagues were determined to be proactive and stay on the front side of the Energy Map. Met said, "We focused on how we could expand the business with them as partners. We told them about our game plan and explained that the dealers need sufficient margins in order to compete and compensate for the costs of stocking and merchandising. We also mentioned that we need to support the dealers with marketing and that this would require additional margins for us. We told them we could expand the business with them if we have sufficient resources. Then we asked them to think about it and tell us what would be workable."

Met and his team stayed focused on the objective and how to get there, and they included in that objective the desire to build stronger relationships with these suppliers. The team was rewarded for its efforts. "After a few days, both suppliers came back to us with lower pricing, thereby increasing margins for us and the dealers. And our relationships with them are stronger than when we started negotiations."

Is it possible that some of the greatest obstacles between a team and its objective are not economically related or market driven but a function of the team's detours to the back side of the Energy Map?

What does your team do to reach its objectives and achieve success rather than becoming locked by goal paralysis?

Top Implications of Focusing on
the Objective and How to Get There:

1. The route to success is formulated internally, not dictated by external factors.

2. Ideas proliferate—and results follow.

3. A Wellness Culture is established with a can-do attitude.

CHAPTER 38

What Using the New Operating System Looks Like

Which Side of the Energy Map Do You Want to Expand?

The preceding chapters show the basic coordinates, the choices everyone around you makes with their focus on the Energy Map. There are, of course, countless other choices, such as:

ENERGY MAP

BACK SIDE		FRONT SIDE
What I don't like about you, me, it	vs.	What I do like about you, me, it
What is wrong?	vs.	What is right?
There isn't enough time	vs.	How do we use the time we have?
Judgment	vs.	Acceptance
Why can't we work together?	vs.	How can we build more trust?
Helplessness	vs.	Responsibility

As we upgrade our individual and collective operating systems, as we function on the front side of the Energy Map more consistently, our lives—and the results we deliver—improve.

The Glass Is Either Getting Emptier —Or Running Over

During a training session, a participant asked, "Isn't the Energy Map just the old routine of the glass being half full or half empty?"

Before the facilitator could respond, another participant's hand sprang up. "No," she said. "It's much more than that. And it's more than simply labeling someone a positive or negative person."

"Why is that the case?" the facilitator asked.

"Because we go toward our focus, we're never sitting still," she said. "If we're on the back side of the Energy Map, we're going to go farther in that direction. If we're on the front side of it, we—and the circumstances in our lives—only get better.

"The Energy Map is much more than a half-empty or half-full glass. Now I know what I'm thinking and the volume of what I'm experiencing never stays still."

Time Well Spent on the Back Side

Is it possible that we *should* occasionally spend time on the back side of the Energy Map?

"Sometimes, in order to get to the front side of the Energy Map, we have to process what's on the back side first," says

E. Renee Franklin, senior vice president of global human resources for Tower Automotive. "Pretending there aren't issues with roots on the back side is negligent behavior. Times like this require extra careful attention and leadership."

An effectively managed sliver of time reserved for the back side of the Energy Map can build trust and cooperation. "Effectively managed" means that back side sojourns are handled in a way that allows people to process emotions and capture lessons and value.

A short trip to the back side of the Energy Map can enable a team to let go of what is holding it back and allow it to move forward again.

If this is not achieved, an elephant will certainly take up residence in the office.

When leaders intentionally take their teams to the back side of the Energy Map, what do those moments look like? We have discussed this with thousands of leaders, and here is what they came up with:

- When emotions such as anger, sadness, disappointment or jealousy are involved, moving forward is impossible until these feelings are let go and processed in a healthy way.

- Some lessons can only be learned on the back side.

- Safety and health issues demand that all data are considered before moving forward.

Questions for Gaining Value
from the Back Side of the Energy Map:

- *"What happened?"* (Asked only if the leader needs more information to formulate forward-focused questions.)

- *"What are you or we experiencing?"* (Asked to identify the emotions involved.)

- *"How did it happen?"* (Rarely asked, but valuable if safety is at stake. Wellness leaders gain the same crucial information but ensure things move forward by asking, "What do we have to do more effectively in the future?" or a similar question.)

- *"What bottlenecks or roadblocks might we anticipate?"* (Risky to ask, because people go toward their focus, but helpful if the leader's intuition says something has not been completely thought through.)

- *"What will you miss about that person?"* (In the event someone leaves, articulating how we feel about this allows us to bring closure and ultimately move forward.)

- *"What would be the cost of doing it that way?"* (Comparing costs with benefits can be a powerful motivator.)

A leader who allows a team to stay on the back side too long, however, can kill the trust, ingenuity and energy an organization needs to thrive. When these qualities have been damaged, the leader cannot patch them up the next morning with flowers and chocolates.

Productivity is a choice; people are productive because they want to be.

Productivity cannot be dictated in an employee policy manual or with larger paychecks. If a leader hampers productivity, even more time and effort are required to redevelop it.

Of course, if the above questions were asked with no follow-up, people would be left to find their own way to the productive, front side of the Energy Map. Such a lack of leadership could have dangerous consequences. Therefore, the next group of questions is designed to follow the preceding questions.

Questions for Leading People
to the Front Side of the Energy Map:

- "What needs to happen now to move us forward in relation to this issue?"

- "What are our new objectives?"

- "What is working that we can build on?"

- "What solutions and execution plans can we consider?"

- "Why are the desired results important?"

- "What can we learn from this incident that will help us in the future?"

Boosting People Boosts the Bottom Line

Kurt Furger, while vice president at a consumer health company, brought a powerful perspective to the topic of the Energy Map. Kurt is a numbers guy. Having spent his career poring over profit-and-loss statements and trying to increase the bottom line, he had earned a reputation using slash-and-burn strategies. At first, he was skeptical about the 3 Mind Factors and the Energy Map approach. Then, when he was introduced to this Wellness Culture approach, he realized it added up.

Asking the facilitator for a moment to comment, he approached a flip chart, drew an Energy Map and added a small box on the back side. Then he drew lines shooting from the bottom of this box, labeling each one as he spoke. "I realize that, for every hour any of us spend on the back side of the Energy Map, we can count on poorer results, higher turnover, lower quality, absenteeism, lack of communication and an un-healthy culture."

Next, he drew an arrow from that box to the front side of the Energy Map, where he drew another box. Adding lines shooting up from this box, he showed his team, "If we move this same hour to the front side of the Energy Map, we get greater results, employee ownership, improved quality, excel-lent customer service, effective communication and a Wellness Culture."

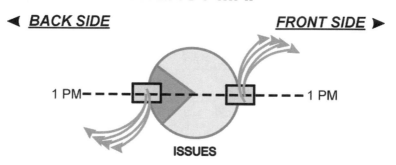

He pointed to the box on the back side of the Energy Map. "We're paying this salary whether the employee is on the back side of the Energy Map or the front." He drew a big dollar sign at the bottom of the flip chart and turned back to his team.

"By boosting our employees, by moving this hour to the front side of the Energy Map, the increase in productivity and results goes directly to the bottom line—because it's not a new expense. It's already been paid for."

Kurt put the pen down and said, "I used to cut things to make the numbers work. But that has to change. I'm here to tell you my job is to move hours to the front side of the Energy Map. That's the number-one way I can help our organization."

The Frontier Your Team
Wants to Explore

What does the terrain of the front side of the Energy Map look like? It is characterized by trust, collaboration, and creativity, but beyond that, the topography is difficult to predict—and that is the point. It is a frontier to which leaders who build Wellness Cultures are constantly guiding their teams because it is the land of solutions and new results. It is where the marketplace is headed. It is a place beyond the comfort zone of average leaders because it is the realm of creation, discovery and self-discipline. Wellness leaders get there before their competition by leading from the front side of the Energy Map.

Readers who use the front side of the Energy Map as their operating system know that once you are in the domain of possibilities, the next stop is endless opportunities.

As employees and teams venture further into the front side of the Energy Map, they experience a euphoric rush. Adrenaline surges as they sense opportunities in every moment. This is where every wellness leader wants his team to be, as often as possible.

Teams do not get to this place of extraordinary results because some leader has tried to be brilliant by having all the answers; nor do they arrive because they were asked to go there through rah-rah rhetoric. Teams, organizations and families get to the front side of the Energy Map because they use Wellness Culture approaches.

Part Seven

HOW TO OPERATE ON THE FRONT SIDE OF THE ENERGY MAP

*Having people around us with
outstanding qualities is not a matter
of giving them those qualities.
It is impossible to give people
what they already have.*

*What type of questions are
you asking yourself? This much is
guaranteed: Your answer reflects
the quality of the results in your life.*

CHAPTER 39

Is Attitude *Really* Just A Matter of Choice?

If It Is That Simple, Why Are So Many Elephants Hanging Around?

There is no time to waste. The demands of business, of life require individuals and organizations to act now; and leaders with the ability to move things forward are in high demand.

The front side of the Energy Map is where results lie. Yet research shows that most individuals and organizations insist on using the least effective operating system—operating on the back side of the Energy Map. This fact is strikingly odd when paired with something every wellness leader understands: Operating on the back or front side of the Energy Map is a matter of choice that *every person has.*

Is it that simple? Is it only a matter of choice whether we move our lives forward or not? If so, why is it so difficult to move forward? Could it be there is something more than the tool called "choice" when it comes to how good we want our life to be or how effective we want to be as leaders?

If we asked 100 people who understand this concept which side of the Energy Map they would choose to operate on, what percentage would respond, "On the front side"? Not only would 100 percent give that response but many of them would think the question was dumb.

Yet the evidence shows that this is not occurring, since 100 percent of people are not operating on the front side of the Energy Map. In fact, the organizational leaders we ask say the percentage is significantly lower than 100—and it is closely related to the disengagement number of 72 percent cited earlier in this book.

The mantra of *choose your attitude* generates limited results.

What does it take to move from the back side of the Energy Map to the front? If simply choosing your attitude is not enough, what is required for people to function more consistently in the space of ideas, solutions and opportunities?

There is a tool that is nearly guaranteed to shift focus and energy to the front side of the Energy Map—and you have access to it right now.

CHAPTER 40

A Wellness Culture Tool: Questions Trigger the Mind

Ask, and You Shall Receive

We would like you to experience this tool before we describe it. To do this we need to ask you an important question first. What time zone are you in right now?

What is your answer?

There. You just experienced firsthand the power of this key understanding: *A little known, seldom used, and powerful fact is that questions trigger the mind.* Questions activate the mind.

When we asked what time zone you are in, your mind either naturally searched for the answer or considered searching for the answer. For a moment, you changed your focus. We have yet to meet a human being who can resist a properly phrased, well-timed question.

Try it. Ask someone near you a relevant question, and observe what happens to his focus. Almost always, the moment you ask a question, his mind starts searching for an answer. To find an answer, the mind has to *focus* on a specific idea or thought.

It is a Wellness Culture truth, a proven piece of leadership technology: Questions trigger the mind. Because every person goes toward his focus, and because you can shift that focus by asking a question, what possibilities does this offer you in your quest to guide others?

Wellness leaders who have put this truth to use over-whelmingly respond with four observations:

1. By asking questions, they can direct a person's focus—including their own.

2. By asking the right types of questions, they can influence a person's attitude, including where that person operates on the Energy Map.

3. By asking questions, they stimulate thinking—including their own.

4. Because they are influencing focus and attitude, these leaders say they now can influence actions and results.

As a leader, what percentage of your time do you spend stimulating thinkers around you? A leader named Gretchen responded this way: "The pace of business today is so fast that we can't spare the time to tell people what to do. They need to be able to think and make decisions for themselves."

Fix-it leaders wait until training sessions to stimulate thinkers or mistakenly use the "telling" approach. This usually backfires because the minds around them shut down. Wellness leaders use a resource that is available countless times every day; they use Magic Moments to build Awareness Muscles, to stimulate thinkers and achieve better decisions. When a Magic Moment presents itself, they often ask questions.

Everyone knows you cannot give leadership skills to others. They have to build those skills themselves. Questions allow them to do that.

"Asking questions releases the clutch on the mind," said Joel LeClair, a leader at the Gerber site in Fremont, Michigan. "It's a method that immediately prompts engagement." Of course, the type of question you ask determines the type of engagement you get.

Is there a chance that we as leaders are actually more responsible for the behaviors and results generated by others than we originally thought?

What would it be worth if, any time you wanted to, you could guide yourself and others to the front side of the Energy Map? This is how to move forward in the toughest areas of Leadership Lock. Asking the right questions exterminates the elephants in our offices and homes. The difference this tool makes can be measured by the bottom lines of numerous organizations and by countless people as they move their lives forward.

How Effective Are You as a Leader?

We can all find new places to use our leadership skills. Some people, however, rationalize their performance as either good or bad on the basis of external circumstances—people, the economy, suppliers—and expect others to change before they can deliver at higher levels. Thankfully, there is a different group of people who know that *their* actions are the key to unlocking the issues they face. Which type of leader are you?

José Tomala, an O-I production manager in Ecuador, is the latter type of leader. The success of his organization is determined by how efficiently he can create high-quality glass products, starting with raw material and ending when bottles reach a pallet. José was raised in a social culture where leaders prove their worth by being "tough and having all the answers." Given this, José knew what had to change in order to create greater results: *his* actions, *his* leadership.

"As we developed our Wellness Culture, people began talking. For example, the guys running the furnace began talking to those beyond the furnace, and the other way around. We stopped saying, 'This isn't my problem. It's their problem.'"

How José achieved this breakthrough provides a clear picture of effective leadership. He said, "When I became plant manager, I wanted to lead the way I had been taught. I thought that all our managers were supposed to be in there telling people what to do, fixing the problems for people, with their sleeves rolled up and getting grease all over them. Then I saw that our guys had some different ideas on how to do things, so I backed off. Instead of forcing my approach, I began asking questions. The ideas we continue to find are what makes us successful."

How successful are they? O-I has plants all around the world. When it comes to efficiency and quality, José's plant went from twenty-fourth in the world to number eleven—and climbing. It has also been recognized as the number-one plant within O-I for the speed with which it can change from producing one type of glass bottle to producing another type. Every minute the line is stopped costs money. José's plant is in the business of making money; José is in the business of leading. He does it with questions.

 Question: How effective are you at leading? Answer: How effective are you at asking questions?

The Elephant-Free Home: House Rules

A soon-to-be stepdad also learned how effective the tools for moving toward the front side of the Energy Map could be. Here is what John Woyak said:

"Before we learned these concepts and tools, my fiancée, Cara, and I thought we would establish some house rules. We had been telling the kids, ages six and five, the rules. But kids will be kids, so we decided to write them down and post them on their bedroom doors. We had five simple rules. I will only share two with you. The first rule was 'Don't Lie' and the second was 'Don't Steal.' Obviously, at the time, we did not know the 3 Mind Factors, including the one that says 'The mind can't avoid a "don't."'"

"Recently, the kids were acting up some at school and at home. Nothing major, but we needed to refocus them. Cara and I used several tools, including the 3 Conditions That Support Change, to have a family talk with the kids. The goal was to have them come up with rules that would work, but in a positive way. Instead of telling, we asked them questions such as 'Who do you love?' 'Why do you love them?' 'What is important to you?' and some others. Through these questions the kids reworked the house rules without us dictating the rules to them. It was pretty neat.

"The first rule is now 'Always tell the truth' and the second is 'Only take what belongs to you.' After we agreed on the rules, the kids wanted to tear up the old rules. They ran upstairs, tore off the sheets from their bedroom doors and ripped them up.

"They're great kids and behave very well. I am so happy to be their future stepdad."

CHAPTER 41

Unplugging the Machine of Progress

Are We the Reason for Poor Performance around Us?

Imagine a worker busy in front of an electric machine. He inserts raw materials at one end of the machine, and a product comes out at the other end. He works in sync with the machine in an effort to produce as many high-quality products as possible, as quickly as he can.

Without warning, the worker's supervisor approaches and unplugs the machine. The supervisor stands erect, arms crossed and a scowl on his face as the engine whines to a halt. The worker is shocked. He glances at the clock on the wall and then at the small stack of products he has produced. The supervisor barks before lumbering off, "Why are you working so slowly? You *have* to reach quota."

Confused, the worker stares at the machine, then frantically plugs it in. He must work faster! The machine chugs into action, and the products start rolling out.

Another day, the supervisor returns. Again he unplugs the machine and stares at the worker intently. The worker nearly stops breathing. Precious time ticks away. The machine is standing still! Eventually, the supervisor shakes his head and points his finger menacingly. "You must ensure lean production. Why are you wasting so many resources?" As the supervisor disappears, the worker lets out a cry. Desperately, he lunges at the power cord, plugs it in and vows to work smarter. The conveyor belt begins to move again.

On another visit, after unplugging the machine, the supervisor picks up a newly built product and moves some of the parts. The worker bites his lip as he hears, "Why is your quality so poor?" Then the supervisor slams the product down and marches off, ordering, "You must quit making mistakes."

For weeks, the supervisor returns. Each time, he unplugs the machine and makes a demand.

One day, after unplugging the machine, the supervisor stands for a longer time than usual, apparently perplexed by the apparatus in front of him. Finally, the worker cannot take it anymore. "Why do you keep unplugging my machine?"

The supervisor looks at the worker and laughs. "This is why you'll never be a supervisor." He unfolded his arms as he pointed at the machine. "I unplugged the machine because I'm trying to figure out what the problem is."

Leaders Who Unplug Their Teams— and Leaders Who Plug Others In

Some leaders, in an effort to improve results, unplug their teams. The questions they ask *destroy* productivity. Because questions trigger the mind and determine focus—and focus leads to direction on the Energy Map—the questions some leaders ask and the "telling" they do disengages members of their team. (This is evidenced by the disengagement data cited earlier in this book.) Some leaders unknowingly sabotage their teams' ability to move things forward. These leaders breed office elephants.

What if you are the worker at the electric machine and you are asked the questions the supervisor asked: Why are you working so slowly? Why are you wasting so many resources? Why is your quality so poor? Why can't you keep up? What makes you think you can handle this job?

What would have happened to your focus with such questions? How would your attitude have shifted? How would these changes have affected your future results?

Here is a results report from a leader who plugged others in: "After a recent project was completed, I was frustrated because our team did not adhere to the timeline we had developed and agreed on. We got the job done, but I wanted to be sure our team was better equipped to hit the deadline next time."

How do you think an average leader would go about accomplishing this? Many would try the traditional "nice work, but . . ." approach, the strategy that contradicts the idea that people want to be great and are capable of raising the bar themselves.

But this leader who plugged others in is not average. Demonstrating what it is like to choose the High Road, she continued: "I had the opportunity to open the next meeting with a question. I asked, 'Now that we have successfully completed our objectives for last quarter, how can we do an even better job this quarter and in the most time-efficient manner?'"

The result: "The question was a big success because my colleagues and my supervisor were open to suggestions and ideas from all the team members—and we found what we needed to improve."

An Awareness Muscle workout: What questions am I asking others? In which direction on the Energy Map am I guiding people? Are my questions developing greater results or destroying them?

CHAPTER 42

A Wellness Culture Tool: Forward-Focus Questions

Drop Leading Questions, and Go with Questions That Lead

Three types of questions determine focus and thus the direction people go on the Energy Map:

1. *Backward-Focus Questions*. These questions lead the focus to the back side of the Energy Map, dragging energy and results backwards as well. These questions are often aimed at short-term, fix-it solutions and typically explore what *has been* rather than what *could be*. Asked repeatedly, they kill enthusiasm, attitudes and momentum. Here are some examples of backward-focus questions:

   - "What's the problem?"

   - "Why isn't this working?"

   - "Why am I such an idiot?"

271

- "Why does this always happen?"

- "What are we doing wrong?"

2. *Neutral Questions.* These questions rely on the person who is answering to determine which direction he will take his focus on the Energy Map. These questions do not determine direction, so they are susceptible to the winds of current attitude. A person with a poor attitude or perspective will answer neutral questions as if they were backward-focus questions. A person with a healthy state of mind will answer neutral questions in a way that moves him and others forward. Here are some examples of neutral questions:

- "How are you doing?"

- "What do you think?"

- "What should I do?"

- "How was your day?"

3. *Forward-Focus Questions.* These questions lead focus to the front side of the Energy Map, naturally moving energy forward. They elicit long-term solutions and focus on building people and processes. They typically explore lessons learned, what is working, and what could be rather than what has been. Asked consistently, they build enthusiasm and momentum. Here are some examples of Forward-Focus Questions:

- "What are you doing that is contributing to the success of this endeavor, and what suggestions do you have for moving things forward more efficiently?"

- "What do you think we can do to move this forward?"

- "What do I want to do that will demonstrate my proficiency in this area?"

- "What was the best part of your day?"

- "What should we do to improve performance?"

Focus the Mind Forward and Ignite Long-term Results

Wellness leaders know that two people can address the same issues—the tough issues, the things that are not working—in different ways and generate different results. Wellness leaders approach all issues in a way that does not involve trying to fix people and problems but helps to develop leaders and create synergy and momentum. They recognize that the issues addressed by the backward-focus questions listed above correspond directly with the issues addressed by the Forward-Focus Questions. Adding only a few key words creates a different focus and thus a different result.

Are you in leadership for the short term or the long term—and are the questions you ask consistent with your answer?

Forward-Focus Questions allow all people to do what it is they want to do—and what it is organizations need them to do: move things forward and get more done.

Socrates Is Thrilled

Using questions to lead, to teach, to move things forward is not a novel idea.

Humans have known for more than two millennia that the best way to engage and teach anyone anything is to ask questions. Socrates practiced this approach over 2,400 years ago. Yet only a select group of schools use this approach, and it is even rarer in the area of leadership—in business or elsewhere. Evidence also indicates that leaders who use questions to move things forward are using only a fraction of the power inherent in the method.

Is it possible that some of the greatest leadership technology available has been lying dormant in a box labeled "common sense"? What happens if we dust it off and, with some courage and persistence, apply it?

For some, asking Forward-Focus Questions requires courage. In addition, ego-driven leaders view questions as a means of exposing that they do not have all the answers—which, ironically, is always the truth. Questions mean they are willing to put someone else in the limelight; questions mean they are willing to explore uncharted waters without the ego crutch of the "I told you so" follow-up.

Elephant-free workplaces are full of leaders who demonstrate this type of courage every day. These wellness leaders are all around us, doing their job, using this fundamental leadership technology to lead and make a difference.

Dan Quigley, an IT expert in the consumer health industry, has put this tool to work by creating his own Forward-Focus formula:

Forward-Focus Questions = Productive Focus

= Positive Attitude = Success

"I've been using mind triggers all along," Dan said. "But I was asking myself and others the wrong questions. It all comes down to the *type* of questions we ask."

Here is an example of how Dan put questions to work: "I turned my concerns into Forward-Focus Questions. In a meeting, for example, instead of saying, 'My fear is that we won't leverage best practices,' I now ask, 'What are your ideas for making sure we leverage best practices?' Not only do I get better results with this approach but the energy is much different."

**It is a fascinating and fail-proof formula
that is worth repeating: Success is determined
by attitude. Attitude is determined by focus.
Focus is determined by the questions
we ask others and ourselves.**

Addressing the Problem
without Focusing on It

The value of asking Forward-Focus Questions is obvious; we are not however, proposing that a leader or parent *never* ask a question exploring information that appears to reside on the back side of the Energy Map. The *method* by which we explore this information is the key.

Craig Ross: "If my daughter is crying, it would be inappropriate to ask, 'But honey, what's the best thing that happened to you today?' I would be asking that to manipulate her to the front side of the Energy Map. Undoubtedly, this would send her further toward the back side."

In this situation, most parents would ask, "What happened?" (A wellness parent knows the difference between that question and "What's wrong?") The issue—why the child is crying—must be identified before the parent can help the child move forward.

The same holds true in organizations. When quality has been compromised, the supervisor cannot jump ahead to the Forward-Focus Question, "What are your ideas for ensuring greater quality in the future?" The timing is not right. Instead, the supervisor will tackle the priority of identifying where things currently stand by asking, "What happened?" (A wellness leader knows the difference between that question and "What's the problem?" or "Whose fault is this?" or "What's not working?")

In these cases, examining the past is necessary to pinpoint the issue that must be moved forward. Gaining a full understanding of the issue without driving the person or team further toward the back side of the Energy Map is the act of a wellness leader or parent with a strong Awareness Muscle. Not coincidentally, these are also people who do not want to create more work for themselves.

Does Communication Mean More "Blah, Blah, Blah"?

The popular saying goes, "If I've told them once, I've told them a thousand times." How long does it take for a person to "get it"? Wellness leaders know the answer: as soon as the person owns it—*as soon as it is the person's idea*. This does not happen by forcing ideas on others. There is a direct link between the elephant in the office and the preferred method of communication: telling. The costs of the "blah, blah, blah" approach:

- *Less engagement around us.* "When he turns his mouth on, we tune out."

- *A greater need for supervision.* "Because everything we do is determined by those who tell us what to do, we're programmed not to move forward without them."

- *Poorer decision making and problem solving.* "Instead of having the brain power of the entire team, we have to rely on a select few for answers. We only hope our competitors are using the same leadership approach."

- *Feelings of being insulted and degraded.* "Just because we have a boss doesn't mean we like to be bossed around. Telling and making demands is the antithesis of the concept that everyone wants to be great."

- *Lower quality.* "Because we're constantly being told, the message has become pretty clear: We're not good enough to do the job ourselves. Would you do your best if that's what you were told over and over?"

Do you know anyone who relies on the outdated communication technology their eighth-grade speech teacher taught?

Sadly, too many people still use the old approach of "Tell them what you're going to tell them, tell them, and then tell them what you told them." This leads to an elephant culture of disengagement and resentment.

Is it possible that, in trying to lower the cost of doing business, a company might overlook the greatest expenditure under its roof—people who rely on the "blah, blah, blah" telling approach? What would happen if people asked Forward-Focus Questions just 10 percent more of the time? How would less telling and more leadership through Forward-Focus Questions help organizations improve the bottom line?

Jaime Ulloa, the business manager of the heavy-duty line for Navistar International in Mexico, demonstrates what is possible—even during a company crisis. "We had a quality issue with a supplier involving 375 trucks that needed to be reworked, and we needed a fast resolution because it was the end of the quarter."

Although many leaders in this type of situation might lose their edge and start "blah, blah, blahing" all over the place, Jaime knew a better route. His efforts reveal his tenacity in taking the High Road.

He said, "At a rework rate of forty minutes per truck, we needed a robust and agile plan to finish by Monday. It was apparent that we'd have to work through the weekend. So my team set up a plan to get going, but I realized it was not enough. With the cycle time planned and the people involved, only seventy-five trucks were going to be fixed.

"To help the team find a solution, all I told them was that our goal had to be getting one hundred percent of the rework done. Then I started asking Forward-Focus Questions. They came up with a better plan, which called for more teams to work two shifts during the weekend. In the end, only nineteen trucks were not finished, and we had enough time during the week to fix them."

Not only did Jaime's team come up with a plan that achieved impressive results but the plan included having teams work through the weekend. Every reader knows that had Jaime demanded this action instead of letting his team members determine their own course, results—including quality—probably would have been disastrous.

Jaime is not a "blah, blah, blah" leader. He and his team demonstrate what happens when a leader uses Forward-Focus Questions to honor the 3 Conditions That Support Change, while knowing that *people want to be great*. It is no surprise that Jaime and his colleagues work at the top-performing plant in their company.

Leading from Your Values

Wellness leaders consider the Humanity Factor to be a driving force behind all they do. They strive to lead from the context of their values and the values of their organizations. They know that acting from a place of integrity, sincerity and compassion is key to achieving superior short- and long-term results. They also realize that using Forward-Focus Questions is an effective way to align their teams with the organization's values.

Nearly every organization has a mission statement, yet the most common approach to giving the mission life within the organization is telling, lecturing, preaching. This approach is akin to giving a dead person CPR.

Telling people what to do and what should be important to them severely damages a leader's effectiveness at aligning a team with the organization's mission and values—and more telling can never bring that effectiveness back.

What is your reaction when someone else tells you what is best for you, how you should function, or how you should view things?

Instead of *forcing* life, wellness leaders *create* life. Forward-Focus Questions allow leaders to more effectively lead from their values and achieve stronger results; instead of merely *talking* about their values, hoping to persuade and thus fix others, wellness leaders *act* according to their values. This builds those they interact with and develops stronger relationships with them.

"Forward-Focus Questions help me lead in the manner I've always believed people should lead, going all the way back to my youth," said Luzia Schlosser, the regional human resources coordinator for O-I Latin America. "I used them in a recent meeting that was getting ugly. We were having problems with a new system that handled payroll. If we didn't get it corrected, we wouldn't make payroll for 1,500 people. In over forty years of business in this region, O-I has never been late paying employees—and I didn't want to be the first person to be late."

Getting this resolved would not be easy. Challenges do not manifest themselves for entertainment purposes; they are a symptom of something that needs resolution. Luzia said, "The first five minutes of the meeting, everyone was pointing fingers. It was a nightmare because everyone was trying to protect themselves. If I didn't do something to change the course of the meeting, it would be a disaster.

"In that Magic Moment, I began asking Forward-Focus Questions geared toward collaboration. I asked the IT representative what was working well in the IT team's interactions with the payroll team, and vice versa. It was difficult for everyone to share answers at first. But slowly, things began to turn around. Instead of blaming each other and fighting, we were slowly moving to the front side of the Energy Map. Then I moved to questions such as, 'What ideas do you have to make this work now?' Instantly, we began to move the issue forward."

Luzia continued, "Occasionally we would slip a bit as people wanted to focus on the problem that had been developing over the past couple of months. In these cases, I would ask another Forward-Focus Question, such as, 'What additional solutions might we consider here?' Each time, with each question, our focus became stronger and more productive.

"Ultimately, we created a perfect solution. It was an intense week—and one of the best of my life as a leader. We closed payroll and paid everybody on time. But the best part was the compliments the different teams were giving each other. Until then, we had been carrying bad relationships born out of past experiences."

Living according to our values is often easier said than done. We can have the *intention* of doing so, only to get frustrated when we discover we do not have the *means* to do so. Luzia's powerful example demonstrates that unlocking her Leadership Lock was not achieved simply by living her values. Nor was it tied solely to her ability to ask Forward-Focus Questions. Rather, she delivered results because of her ability to use these powerful questions in combination with other Wellness Culture tools.

She explained, "First, I had to move to the front side of the Energy Map myself. I love people. Still, sometimes it's not easy to deal with others. I have to take a Magic Moment before each meeting.

"And I'm growing my Awareness Muscle by learning to give people time to determine *how* they can change. I'm learning that each person has a different time frame to choose how to do things differently. By using questions to fulfill the 3 Conditions That Support Change, I am getting better at bringing us all together to produce the results everybody wants."

By using the Wellness Culture tools, Luzia is discovering something else as well. "I'm learning that people wake up and want to give the best they can. As I learn this, it inspires me to help them give their best."

These are values Luzia has. Because she is living them, she brings more value to others and to her organization.

The Genius Behind Forward-Focus Questions

In advance of a Pathways to Leadership® session at a consumer health organization, a senior leader observed: "If we had employees with strong self-esteem, confidence, fully participating and excited about the work they have to do, we'd have it made."

"Why would you have it made?" the facilitator asked.

"Because most of the problems that slow us down would disappear," the leader responded. "But the question is: How do you get your employees there?"

News flash: What if those around you, in their natural state, are *already* there? What if some of us have been trying to give others something they already have? People often lack strong self-esteem, confidence and enthusiasm because those around them have assisted in taking these traits away from them.

Having people around us with outstanding qualities is not a matter of giving them those qualities. It is impossible to give people what they already have. Our job is to create an environment—a Wellness Culture—in which they can deliver what they naturally have.

Leaders who have seen the results concur: There is no better way to build self-esteem, help team members discover their own brilliance, and give them the satisfaction of contributing to the team's results than by asking Forward-Focus Questions. Here is a sampling of what such questions look like:

- "Where have you experienced great results that you can apply to this situation?"

- "What is your vision for this project?"

- "What are the reasons you feel you are capable of achieving our objectives?"

- "Why is the outcome important to you?"

Wellness leaders agree: There is no better way to help people become effective, confident leaders and to provide opportunities for them to discover their own solutions than by asking Forward-Focus Questions like these:

- "What do you feel are the critical factors we need to be aware of and explore as we address this situation?"

- "What will it take for you to pull this off brilliantly?"

- "What have you discovered in past situations that you want to apply here?"

- "What data will you use to measure your progress?"

Effective people are convinced: There is no better way to foster enthusiastic collaboration than by asking team members their vision for the team, how they want to contribute and work together, and why that is important to them:

- "If our team can become the most effective, dynamic team in the company, how would you like to see us operate?"

- "In what ways would you like to see our team members support each other?"

- "Why is it important to you to be part of a great team?"

- "What are the characteristics of this team that you feel will allow us to accomplish our goals?"

A wellness leader in Memphis, Tennessee, faced a significant challenge. Using questions, he delivered his strategy and better results. He said, "My challenge was to manage and build a team after the previous manager was removed from the company. I used Forward-Focus Questions to establish an open flow of communication and set clear objectives. We developed guidelines and a strategy to get there.

"As a result, we are rebuilding the trust and respect of our business partners. The team members are working together well. We've been able to ship $100 million in new product, and a $1.9 million capital project that was four months late is now scheduled to be delivered on time and on budget."

**This leader quickly discovered that
Forward-Focus Questions generate solutions.
They are a tool that honors the 3 Conditions
That Support Change and builds the
pillars of a Wellness Culture.**

There is a yet-unstated benefit to the approach of Forward-Focus Questions that wise readers will have noted. Like the leader in the example above, those who use Forward-Focus Questions not only deliver a stronger bottom line for the organization; not only do they develop trust, rapport, collaboration and synergies; they also do something that will reverberate throughout the organization for years to come: They expand the capabilities of the people around them. They develop leaders who will continue to create an elephant-free workplace.

CHAPTER 43

Stomp the Elephant In the Office by Eliminating Leadership Blind Spots

Elephants Hide Here and Prey on Strategies

Jim, a mid-level manager at a large international company, arrives at his office by 6:30 A.M. every day and leaves at 7:00 P.M. His direct reports, who work down the hall, are accountable and productive. Jim is on time for every meeting, and he reads most of the memos and e-mails he is copied on. He knows what is happening in his industry. He is on top of the status of every project, upcoming challenges and the latest figures and results. Because of this, many might think Jim is effective at keeping office elephants at bay.

What we do not know, however, can hurt us. Recently, Jim was "surprised and devastated" when Sally, one of his top performers, submitted her resignation. He knew this would hurt his department's performance, and he later confessed it could hurt his career, too.

Jim now admits he suffered from a disease that runs rampant with leaders. He knew what his staff members were doing, but he did not know what they were thinking and experiencing.

Here is what Jim knew about Sally's performance: She arrived at work on time; her projects and assignments were executed flawlessly and usually delivered ahead of schedule; and the entire team enjoyed being around her.

On the other hand, these were Jim's leadership blind spots about Sally:

- Why her work was important to her.

- How she felt about working with the team.

- What else she might like to learn and do.

- In what areas she might be able and willing to contribute more creative energy and accelerate results.

- How he might help her achieve her goals and enhance her career.

- How satisfied she was with her work.

"It was as if I was trying to lead with a blindfold on," Jim confessed. "The only thing I was concerned about was how my team was performing. Then, out of nowhere, Sally springs the news on me." Out of nowhere, an office elephant stomped on Jim.

He said: "I didn't realize Sally felt the way she did. I didn't have a clue as to what she was thinking. I gave myself a leadership handicap."

Like the leader who reads only spreadsheets or who unplugs machines to figure out why the operator is unproductive, Jim was leading with limited information. He was making leadership decisions based on his employees' work, not on information about the employees doing the work. In a world of cause and effect, he was trying to manipulate the effect without influencing the cause. He was not leading. To a certain degree, he was following.

How effective are you at garnering—and using—the type of information that remains in many leaders' blind spots?

Average leaders wait until their employees' yearly one-hour performance reviews to gain the information sitting in their blind spots—if they do it at all. Wellness leaders know they cannot eliminate leadership blind spots in a one-hour-per-year conversation. Instead, wellness leaders gain such information whenever the opportunity arises and when it is appropriate. They use Magic Moments throughout the year to ask questions. Sometimes these moments last only seconds, and when they use them these leaders develop 20/20 leadership vision.

Leaders with 20/20 vision create greater results. José Chacon is the executive president of Navistar Financial Service in Mexico City. His objective is to build a world-class financial organization, and with a growing business, he is on his way. "This concept has made a big difference," he reported.

"How others feel is important to me because how they feel determines how they act. Now I'm listening for their feelings. This is a more natural process; I'm no longer imposing my feelings."

How valuable is it for you to know what is important to others? Having access to the information stored in leadership blind spots affects your ability to reach your business objectives.

Accomplishing 20/20 Leadership Vision

Do you believe you can see all the elephants around you? How valuable is it for you to know what is important to others? Having access to the information stored in leadership blind spots affects your ability to reach your business objectives.

As you saw in part five, wellness leaders know their team members want to be great. These leaders know they need information found in blind spots in order to help others evolve from good to great, in order to make service-oriented leadership a reality. They also know something Jim had to discover in a painful fashion.

**When employees' questions and desires
are explored, considered and acted on,
they rarely go looking for different jobs.**

Knowing leadership blind-spot information is vital to short- and long-term results. Knowing how to garner this information in an effective, healthy way is the challenge accepted by wellness leaders.

Of course, observing someone's behavior is one way to identify blind-spot information, but this passive approach can lead to misinterpretations. So how does a leader gain the information he needs to know? The answer: by asking Forward-Focus Questions.

Here are some sample Forward-Focus Questions Jim could have asked to eliminate his leadership blind spots about Sally:

Blind Spot: Why her work was important to her.

Sally, what are the reasons this project is important to you? In what ways does this work align with your career objectives? How do you feel this project will help our team with its goals?

Blind Spot: How she felt about working with the team.

Sally, what are some of the qualities you appreciate about our team? How would you like to see our team stretch and grow? What difference do you feel the proposed action plan will make for our team and its objectives?

Blind Spot: What else she might like to learn and do.

Sally, how would you like to grow in your career? What is the reason this growth is important to you? How can I support you?

Blind Spot: In what areas she might be able and willing to contribute more creative energy and accelerate results.

Sally, what are your ideas for taking this project to an even higher level of efficiency and results? What are some other sources we can tap for ideas to help us move forward more effectively?

Blind Spot: How he might help her achieve her goals and enhance her career.

Sally, how do you feel things are going with your career? What are some specific aspects that you feel are going well? What are some of your aspirations for the future? What kind of support would you like from me?

Blind Spot: How satisfied she was with her work.

Sally, in what areas are you satisfied with your work? With our work together? With our team? What are some of your frustrations? What are some of your ideas on how we can collaborate to make things even better in the future?

On the exit survey conducted by the human resources department, Sally gave the following reason for leaving her employment: *"I didn't feel connected to the rest of my team. I never felt as if my ideas made a difference. There's no momentum and enthusiasm here."*

Only a rare conversation would allow a person to address numerous blind spots at once; with proper timing, the essentials can gradually be covered. Effective leaders trust their intuition in determining what blind-spot information can be solicited through questions and what information will likely remain private. Still, through eliminating leadership blind spots, they make building relationships a priority.

Dan McRae is the general manager for Caraustar Custom Packaging Group in St. Louis, Missouri. His plant is one of the most efficient and productive in the company. It did not get that way by accident. Dan is a wellness leader who uses the Wellness Culture tools to eliminate leadership blind spots.

He explained, "We open our production meeting every morning with a Forward-Focus Question. This meeting opener gets us all connected and engaged and reminds us we're a team.

"We rotate responsibility for opening the meeting with this type of question. Last week someone asked, 'What do you value most about Caraustar–St. Louis?' The question seemed simple at first. The answers focused primarily on our relationships and what we value most about our teammates. By the time we made it around the table, a couple of people were in tears and a few others were choking them back. It was clear that major changes had taken place in the way we view our workplace.

"Our emphasis on a Wellness Culture has given us a sense of teamwork and common ground. Our group is mature, but we were missing the common ground that is truly needed. This approach has given us the missing element that has made us a highly effective team in which everyone is valued. The results are evident from our bottom-line performance over the past two years. We expect continued success at St. Louis because our people are empowered with the gifts of teamwork and trust."

Dan McRae's team is doing something average people do not do: It is achieving 20/20 leadership vision by eliminating leadership blind spots; there are no office-elephant tracks because people are investing time in building individual and team wellness upstream, so they do not have to waste time fixing things downstream. They understand that they are humans with needs, desires, opinions and attitudes; and they have the fortitude and leadership tools to address that humanness effectively.

CHAPTER 44

The Person the Office Elephant Fears Most

It Is Your Turn

You know that people who effectively lead others must first lead themselves. Leadership wannabes with underdeveloped Awareness Muscles need not apply for positions that demand results.

Take a close look at your life. The direction you are headed, the results you are generating are not an accident. Because questions trigger the mind, the questions we ask ourselves determine our thoughts. Our thoughts drive our attitudes, and, of course, our attitudes determine our results. How many of us consciously and effectively lead ourselves? How significant is it that we are guided by the types of questions we ask ourselves?

All of us know people who are leading themselves nowhere by asking themselves "garbage questions." Garbage questions in, garbage results out. It is a special person who takes the direction of his life into his own hands.

"Tough things will happen in my life," said Susan Morava of the Hemingford Cooperative Telephone Company in Nebraska. "By asking the right questions, I can handle those things on the front side of the Energy Map and still go forward.

"Before, when things would get tough, I would ask, 'Why me?' or 'What's wrong with me?' or 'Why are they so stupid?' Looking back, I see how much worse these garbage questions made things. Now I ask, 'What are the most important lessons I can learn from this? What outcome do I want to create, and what are the smartest ways to go about achieving it? How can I use this situation to raise the bar and produce even better results?' No surprise, the results have been impressive."

Some people let the circumstances of their lives determine their focus and thus their attitudes and results. But there is another type of person whose ranks are increasing: people who create their futures by asking themselves Forward-Focus Questions.

What type of questions are you asking yourself? This much is guaranteed: Your answer reflects the quality of the results in your life.

When we ask ourselves Forward-Focus Questions, and apply the other Wellness Culture tools, we do more than lead ourselves. With consistent application, we increasingly find ourselves grounded in the bedrock of our principles and values. From this, our actions become a natural outgrowth of the Humanity Factor.

Now we invite you to read the next part of this book again, with brand new eyes. At this point you not only have the dream and the passion but also confidence and tools to execute your strategy, to deliver your dream.

The elephants in your life do not have a chance. Go ahead, stomp them.

Part Eight

THE
HUMANITY
FACTOR

*Moving through a day without
making a difference in the
lives around us results in an
immeasurable loss of
human potential.*

*Wellness leaders celebrate
the human spirit in
everything they do.*

CHAPTER 45

What Is Your Reason for Doing What You Do? (And Is That Reason Making a Difference?)

When you opened your eyes this morning, were you excited? Were you eager to experience what would lie ahead in the next twenty-four hours? Were you centered and at ease?

Two types of people answer yes to these questions. The first are people who know what they want to achieve. They have a vision for what is possible and are going for it. They are motivated and will most likely create the results they want. Yet they will still experience inconsistency; they still face mornings of dread, unease and frustration.

The second type who answer yes are in an entirely different class.

These people have been able to sustain the momentum of enthusiasm and peacefulness in their lives because of one reason: What they want to achieve for themselves in life also benefits others. This approach changes everything—for the individual and for all of humanity.

297

This latter approach is called the Humanity Factor: when people care about other human beings so much that it influences their interactions. When people use the Humanity Factor, it lifts how they relate with every person they come into contact with, because they have an accountability outside of self. The result is immediately and consistently visible as it influences thoughts, actions and outcomes for the better.

The Impact of the Humanity Factor

Each of us wants to make a difference. Yet surprisingly few of us use the Humanity Factor. There are people who go through their entire lives looking for the chance to make a difference. Then there is also a group of people who wake up and know that within *every day* they will find countless opportunities to deliver on this urge.

Leaders use the Humanity Factor on two levels. Both levels contain the seeds of monumental change:

1. When we personally reconnect to our vision, our dream, and we remember that we can and do affect the lives of others by how we act, it influences how we manage every minute of our day. For some, this approach clarifies their purpose for living.

2. When we function in a way that provides *others* with the opportunity to implement the Humanity Factor—to make a difference in other people's lives—it moves people and organizations into a realm of uncommon productivity and influence in the world community. This approach allows many to live their dream of leadership.

A Call to Who We Were—and Who We Are

Freddy Vallejo knows the Humanity Factor. He knows it because he forgot it, and then rediscovered it with new eyes.

A mid-level manager, Freddy said, "Growing up I had a lot of dreams. I was excited about everything I wanted to do. Also, as I worked through my first few jobs, I quickly learned I didn't want to be like the bosses I had. Many in the older generation seemed so negative about everything.

"And something else was clear. I knew I would do something special with my life. I would make a difference. My work would be meaningful and fulfilling for me and everyone around me. By doing this, I figured there would be a lot of joy in everything I did—including the time I was with my family."

There is something that binds us all together. In every person there once was, and in some cases still is, the desire to make a difference in the lives of others. When we heard about the harmful acts and poor decisions made by others, we proudly proclaimed that we would be different; we would, whenever given the chance, conduct our lives in a way that would benefit others. We may not have known what we wanted to be, but we knew what we wanted to do. Do you remember?

"I've had a big wake-up call. With increased awareness, I realize that I've traded in my dreams. I hate to say this, but in many ways, I think I quit on myself. What's alarming is it all changed so subtly; day after day I lowered my expectations. I'd wake up every morning while it was still dark and move around the house like a robot. It was time to face another day of the grind: raised voices and short words with the kids and wife in the morning. Run out the door by six o'clock. The same pointless meetings and demands at work. Then at night sit in traffic behind people who don't know how to drive, just to get home and take on an endless list of things to do. After that, play nice and finally get angry with the kids who never get to bed on time. And when the lights begin to go out, clench my teeth while doing e-mails that are long overdue. At some point close to midnight, I try to numb out the frustration so I can get some sleep."

Freddy took a deep breath. "The dreams I had when I was young were long gone. In fact, I was falling further behind."

Was it all a grand illusion? Was the idea that we could make money and make a difference in the lives of others a lie? The temptation to subscribe to false information and beliefs is strong. It is tempting to believe we need to have a certain job or make a certain amount of money to serve others. When we look at the evidence, however, we know we have fooled ourselves: Despite the jobs we have had and the money we have earned, the hunger to know our lives have not been lived in vain remains.

A hunger left unchecked can lead to fatigue, cowardice and forfeiture. For some of us, just like Freddy, we slowly let the dream go. We did the math: The pressures we faced to feed our families, to have the cars we wanted, to pay the mortgage, to get the kids to camp and through college, or to get the coveted office with a view—all these demands were increasing rapidly even though we had lost our excitement for them. Almost without notice, our dreams were transformed into fantasies, and the enthusiasm of a morning faded into discontent and fear of failure.

So some of us concluded we would not make a difference during our lifetime. Forfeiting a dream is not easy, but we rationalized that being able to make a difference in other people's lives was reserved for those whose occupations allowed them to do so—ministers, teachers, counselors, therapists, doctors, and so forth.

Like boats pushed into the fog without rudders, we left the solid ground of our values, principles and dreams for an uncharted course over a sea of false hopes. One day washed into the next, until some of us were so far away from the shore of our values and dreams that we could no longer see them. With this loss of vision we also lost some other things—colors were no longer as bright and laughter was no longer as loud.

Freddy, however, is not your average leader. Finding himself in such a sea, he did not wait for a leader above him or a friend beside him to change his circumstances. Instead of buying the common approach that says a person has to change his circumstances to be happy, Freddy did not change many things at all.

All he changed was Freddy. In addition to using the leadership tools in this book, he did something else. He used a tool that altered his attitude when he woke up in the morning, transformed his actions and changed how he led. He used the Humanity Factor.

"Remembering that I had that dream, the desire to make the world a better place, is now changing everything for me. It's changing how I go about my day. And as a result, I am beginning to have that feeling again: that my life counts for something, that my actions are making a difference."

He shrugged his shoulders. "I'd forgotten that I had that dream. But I remember now—and I know it's possible. I am living proof that you can be miserable and get poor results— and by changing your approach you can change your results.

"I still go to the same job, sit in the same traffic, have the same wife, kids, dog and house. But I see them differently. Now, they all seem like blessings. Because I see them differently, I deal with them differently. The objective is no longer what can I get but what can I give."

These days, with his peers, customers and family, Freddy is a wellness leader who is making a difference. He has gotten out of the trap of thinking he needs a different job; that his company should make a different product; or that he has to write a book, start a nonprofit organization, or volunteer overseas in order to make a difference in this world. Instead, with every communication and interaction with others, Freddy builds people and relationships and moves issues forward. Every day he makes a difference.

"I am happy again, excited again. And this approach is becoming automatic. When the alarm goes off, I no longer think about how bad I have it or ask myself how I can get out of all the stupid meetings on my calendar. Instead, I ask myself how I can make a greater contribution in the day ahead. I ask myself how I can use my strengths and talents to make a difference."

The Humanity Factor is a leadership upgrade that costs nothing to implement, and it provides immediate results. This factor instantly begins to create an elephant-free culture and has an impact on the bottom line. Freddy and countless other leaders around the world are achieving these results by reconnecting with their purpose, thereby answering a higher calling in their leadership work.

 When you were younger, were you convinced that you too were born to make a difference? Have you ever dreamed that your work would make the world a better place?

The World's Perfect Job
(Hint: You Have Already Applied for It)

Freddy demonstrates a priceless component of the Humanity Factor. When work—any work—is done right, it is never solely about making money. It is also not only about making a difference. Our job, whatever it is, is the most important lifetime vehicle for our own maturation, growth, evolution and happiness.

When we create the right relationships at work and have the right ongoing conversations with others and ourselves— conversations that include what we want to contribute and receive from our work—our job becomes a vehicle for our life journey. Then we have the perfect job for us.

Whether we are driving a truck, flying to the moon, inspecting a spreadsheet, leading a thousand people or leading one—our work becomes part of a pilgrimage to discover who we are as people, what we stand for, who we want to be, why that is important, and how we get there. The Humanity Factor helps us on that journey. The Humanity Factor makes any job the perfect job.

CHAPTER 46

The World Is Calling For Our Best Efforts

Opportunities Are Waiting for Us Everywhere

Research on leadership effectiveness provides overwhelming evidence to indicate that dramatic changes are needed.

- Of Americans, 62 percent believe leaders are primarily out to enrich themselves monetarily, while 72 percent believe the United States will decline as a nation unless we find better leaders (from a 2005 study by Harvard's Center of Public Leadership and *U.S. News and World Report*).

- Only 17 percent of working people say they spend most of their day doing things they like, reports Marcus Buckingham in the August 2005 issue of *Fast Company*.

- Workers report that two out of five days are a waste of time, Microsoft Corporation discovered after conducting an online survey of 40,000 people from 200 countries.

- Workers clock an average of 45 hours per week but consider about 17 of those hours unproductive, reports the March 15, 2005, online edition of *Information Week*.

Most of you do not need these statistics to convince yourselves of the growing demand for innovation in the way we lead others and ourselves. Most of us have observed the evidence firsthand. We have seen the emptiness in the eyes and actions of our coworkers—people wanting something more. At the dinner table and in our conversations with friends, we hear about office politics, endless meetings, boredom and lack of trust. We hear about people fighting for bonuses and promotions while struggling to make their rent or mortgage payments. Then, sadly, too many do not realize satisfaction even when they can make those payments.

Far too many organizations, small and large, sabotage the health of society by acting as breeding grounds for negativity and mediocrity.

In the worst cases, some organizations have become spores of illness, creating a burden for the public through lawsuits, emotional and physical health issues, and episodes of violence.

What are the costs when leaders push for business results first and then try to find a few days on the calendar to move humanity forward? Who wins in the long run—organizations that make serving their colleagues and community an equal priority with serving their clients and stockholders, or organizations that do not?

In some situations, it seems companies are simply paying people for the hours of their lives they are willing to sacrifice. Consequently, people are upset because they would rather be paid for *something else*.

What is that something else? Leaders who guide a Wellness Culture know it so well, it determines how they use every leadership tool available to them. It is the factor that determines how successful they ultimately are. It is the Humanity Factor.

By emphasizing the Humanity Factor, we become leaders at every point in our lives—when we are pumping gas, in a meeting, ordering take-out, or kissing our children good night.

The Humanity Factor allows us to leverage every moment for greatness. It allows us to make a difference. This is leadership.

This undeniable passion to serve others connects us to our fellow man. Because this factor is consistent across communities and continents, it reveals a universal certainty: High-quality leadership is how we can realize this common purpose.

Many people already know this. The Humanity Factor is the reason they do what they do. It is the reason they go to work every day.

What Will Happen If You Use the Humanity Factor

If you use the Humanity Factor, people will come to you. They will follow you. If you use the Humanity Factor so people will follow you, they will not. You already know why.

A Case Study:
Building Something Worth Fighting For

A group of leaders was discussing the number of disengaged employees in their company and lamenting the current state of the workforce.

"I know a person we all perceive as disengaged," Sherri said. "Mindy." The others in the room nodded in agreement.

"What's interesting, though," she continued, "is that Mindy is one of the most active members of our church, she's on the school board, and she volunteers a lot of her time with numerous service organizations."

The room was quiet. Then Sherri continued. "I'm wondering how many of our disengaged employees are disengaged because we've *made* them disengaged?"

At this, Bill, another supervisor, spoke up. "But Sherri, you just said it yourself. She's engaged at church and in the community—those are all causes worth fighting for. This is work."

The room was silent as everyone waited to see who would respond. It was their senior leader. "What are you saying, Bill?"

Bill looked down at the table for a moment, then looked up and chuckled. "Actually, I want to recant what I just said." He looked at Sherri. "We need to create a workplace that gives Mindy something to fight for right here."

The World Has Its Heroes.
Now It Needs You

Is it possible for us to tap into the motivations of others so effectively that people will bring their passion, enthusiasm and commitment to what they do? Or is this type of leadership reserved for people like Lincoln, Gandhi, Martin Luther King Jr. and Mother Teresa?

Obviously not. These heroes were effective because they inspired people to greater action. People changed their behaviors because they had good reason to: the common good of humankind. These icons galvanized others through various means. They, like the wellness leaders who are creating exceptional and sustainable organizational results, had at least one common characteristic:

They worked not to glorify themselves but to glorify the purpose. The purpose was improving conditions for humankind. That is the Humanity Factor in action.

When a person knows his life is meaningful and he can make contributions through his efforts at work, then his work is no longer a drain on his energy. On the contrary, his work adds significantly to each day. The work does not take over his life but complements it.

Is it possible that ridding our rooms, our homes, our offices of elephants is not as difficult as we have imagined it to be? Is it possible that we have made leadership more difficult than it needs to be?

There Will Be Doubters. How Will You Respond?

Will there be naysayers? Will there be those who doubt society can have workplaces that contribute to the well-being of each employee and the communities they live in? Certainly. But wellness leaders do not invest their time in addressing the question, "Is it a possibility?" These leaders know the real question is, "How do we make this vision a greater reality?"

It is already becoming a reality. For example, Ford of Mexico has been using this approach for over four years and has seen its employee satisfaction numbers jump over 25 percent to reach 89 percent. Not surprisingly, Ford of Mexico is leading Ford's worldwide recovery, as you read earlier.

Rick Popp said, "With the Humanity Factor, we can truly demonstrate that we care about the whole person. As a leader, I can feel I'm doing something special. I'm not just developing this person for work."

Will there also be people who do not seem to possess this factor, this desire to serve and make a difference? You know there will be. In such cases, we are usually tempted to tell such people that they—their beliefs and their actions—are wrong.

Beware. Such an approach moves the person in question even further away from the fundamental core: the natural desire to use the Humanity Factor. Few people embrace being wrong. When informed that we are wrong, many of us double our efforts to prove our beliefs and actions are right. Only by knowing that all people, even those we doubt, possess this core value—only by using the Humanity Factor ourselves—can we move everyone forward.

How do we move our organizations even more toward the day when everyone shows up for work and says, "I stand for something. My life is about making a difference"?

**How do we as leaders make a difference
so profound that the people around us
also live better lives?**

Wellness leaders know the answer is to incorporate the Humanity Factor into their own leadership and make it the bedrock of their Wellness Culture. This is what it looks like:

- These people lead people first, while they manage spreadsheets. Spreadsheets cannot move an organization or society forward, and they cannot smile at a client. Wellness leaders know that leading themselves and others is the priority.

- These people approach their jobs as opportunities to add value; to help colleagues move forward; to become better team members, citizens and family members; and to make life more enjoyable for others.

- The tombstones of these leaders will not show: "I made a lot of money and got six promotions." Instead, their epitaphs will read something like: "Loving spouse, parent, and businessperson who served his community and made a difference in the world."

CHAPTER 47

The Humanity Factor Changes Everything

It Starts by Changing the Way You Think

"The power of the Humanity Factor is that it changes the way you think," said Mark Cicotello, vice president of human resources for the Heska Corporation in Loveland, Colorado. "When you change the way you think, you change the way you act. And when you change the way you act, you change outcomes. This changes our destiny and prepares us for the future."

When Will Your Future Change?

Have you ever known someone who forfeited today waiting for circumstances to change before making his move? This behavior marks the difference between those who run with elephants, and those who function in elephant-free environments.

Wellness leaders know that, because of the Humanity Factor, there is only one time to make a difference—*now*. Average people often wait a lifetime to make a difference. But wellness leaders, whether they are Joan the CEO or Joe the janitor, do not fall into the trap of leading only at certain moments or in the presence of certain people. Wellness leaders honor the Humanity Factor all the time. Their influence on others and results is significant.

Instead of leading only when confronting a challenge, they also lead before and after the challenge appears. They use the Humanity Factor because it is the right thing to do, because it is who they are. As a result, they face fewer challenges themselves, find better solutions, and help others—indeed, the world—overcome their challenges.

You Can Be Effective
Any Time You Want To

Recently, a woman told us about her experience of grocery shopping with a friend. "The entire time we were together, my friend complained about all the things she had to do, all the troubles in her life, and how the stress was affecting her. Finally, as we walked through the parking lot, she said, 'It never ends. It just never ends!' That's when I looked at her, smiled, and said, 'You're right. It never ends.'"

Leadership never ends. There will always be challenges that must be addressed. Effective leaders capitalize on the challenges they are presented because they see these issues as a call to innovate, a call to take themselves and those around them to a higher level. They do this in a way that enhances the quality of life for everyone.

Because the Humanity Factor instantly enriches your experience and increases your effectiveness, your leadership abilities are amplified. Because the choice to implement the Humanity Factor is nobody else's decision, and because nobody else can take away your ability to use it, you can use it any time you choose. You can become a more effective leader as quickly as you can take a breath.

For some people, not making the decision to act with the Humanity Factor, not realizing the dream they have of making a difference, would cripple them. Persevering in this endeavor is what their life's work has become.

Moving through a day without making a difference in the lives around us results in an immeasurable loss of human potential.

Undoubtedly, you realize that wellness leaders must sometimes take a more challenging road to achieve results. In environments where there are elephants in the room, where a Wellness Culture has not been established, it is more popular to complain, to be helpless and negative than to stand up for what works and what is possible.

Even in the face of such adversity, wellness leaders function differently. Not only do they know what is right but they also have the courage to do and say what is right. They do not wait for a glorious moment when they can be heroic in the eyes of others. Instead, they have the courage to step up and move forward in every moment of every day. They have the courage to provide daily leadership in uncommon and quietly heroic ways.

This Is Like No Other Time in History

As we focus on our desire to make a difference, we need to bear in mind two things:

1. Undoubtedly, most of us are making a difference in the world already. Every day we seize moments to serve—either through words or simple actions. We care, and others know we care.

2. At the same time, we have the opportunity to make an even greater difference in the world. As the global economy expands, organizations are influencing society worldwide and affecting the quality of life of nearly every person on the planet. In this international community we are all becoming more dependent on one another.

As organizations expand the sphere in which they do business, millions of interactions, including e-mails and phone calls, take place daily. Imagine if the Humanity Factor and other leadership tools were embedded in these communications. Like no other time in history, right now channels of influence are opening up that will allow each of us to make a profound difference in the quality of life on Planet Earth.

**Consider the possibility that as leaders
take innovative steps forward in how they lead,
progress with the world's major challenges—
hunger, poverty, peace, education, preservation
of the environment—will also move forward
more rapidly. It is clear: Only leadership can
change the world.**

Consider that advances in leadership begin with us. Each one of us is a leader on this planet. If we are not interacting with someone who is communicating on an international level, chances are we are only two or three conversations removed from someone who is.

Wellness leaders celebrate the human spirit in everything they do. These people are artists, sculpting masterpieces where unaligned teams once stood; they are tacticians who deftly bring focus and common cause where rivals once fought; they are musicians creating harmony where chaos once reigned; they are engineers who build bridges of faith and hope into tomorrow where despair was once rampant. These are the people all around you who know the human spirit's desire to serve mankind reveals itself in infinite ways.

Using the Humanity Factor transforms the task of leadership into an opportunity for which each of us has been called. How will you lead, moment by moment, so that you can do what everyone inherently wants to do? How will you make a difference?

The expanding world of wellness leadership welcomes all of our contributions.

EPILOGUE

Integration and sustainability in any change effort is as important as, if not more important than, the initial effort. A true Wellness Culture is not only sustainable but becomes a way of life. Since the early drafts of this book, things have changed for those whom you have read about.

The leaders highlighted in this book, and the companies and teams they are a part of, continue to apply the tools and the Wellness Culture approach we describe in these pages. Consequently, the results they generate continue to evolve as well.

For updates—to discover the extraordinary things these leaders have learned and what they have achieved—visit www.stomptheelephant.com. Current, specific applications of how they used the tools highlighted in *Stomp the Elephant in the Office* can also be found. In addition, free tools and strategies on how you can build your Wellness Culture can be downloaded at your convenience.

Also, we would like to hear from you. It is through our combined efforts and the leveraging of each other's wisdom that we can truly deliver on the promise of who we each are as leaders. We welcome your questions, challenges, successes and thoughts at steveandcraig@verusglobal.com.

APPENDIX A

Strategies for Successful
Elephant-Stomping Groups

Creating an elephant-free office or community requires intentional actions. Elephant-stomping groups are a proven method to putting an end to the toxic workplace, getting more done and creating excitement about work again. Essentially, these groups are leadership forums that assist people and teams to deliver better results by enhancing their ability to use the tools highlighted in this book.

Elephant-stomping groups are being conducted around the world—and delivering the sorts of results you have read about in this book. Below is the information you need to start your own group and lead it successfully.

What results can we expect as we participate in elephant-stomping groups?

Synergies will increase as people form a common language in their leadership efforts. The tools and strategies in this book make their way deep into the workplace, allowing people and teams to execute strategies faster. As the Wellness Culture grows, results accelerate and the bottom line improves.

How many people should be in each elephant-stomping group?

It is best to create teams consisting of three to eight people. This allows everyone to have a voice; the small number also is conducive to generating breakthrough synergies.

Who should be included in each group?
You can approach this in one of three ways.

1. All or part of an entire team that is already functioning well—and that wants to create even greater results—can use this format.

2. Elephant-stomping groups are a proven vehicle to break down the walls between people and departments—walls that create safe havens for elephants. We encourage you to invite people with whom you want to build stronger relationships. As these relationships grow stronger, elephants flee the premises.

3. You can also invite respected peers from other organizations, peers you want to serve and develop a relationship with.

How often should the elephant-stomping groups meet?
Weekly meetings are the most popular and effective format. Numerous organizations, however, create stellar results hosting the meetings bimonthly or monthly. On average, the meetings last forty-five minutes to one hour. Most groups meet four to eight times. Some organizations leverage this process so well that the elephant-stomping groups meet continuously. In these cases, they periodically shuffle participants and consistently rotate business applications.

Is this just a book study format?
No. Simply put, the elephant-stomping groups are designed to help you do your business—better. This book, *Stomp the Elephant in the Office*, and the leadership tools within it are a support mechanism to that end; therefore, meeting moderators will assign specific pages or sections for participants to read in advance.

What do the group meetings look like?

What follows is a basic sample agenda. Expanded agendas and support documents are available for free on the Internet at our Web site, www.stomptheelephant.com.

- Meeting Opener: Where have we seen leadership that has eliminated elephants in our area lately—and allowed us to get more done?

- Where have we been executing our strategies effectively?

  - How have we been achieving that?

- From the recommended reading, what portions do you feel were most important?

  - Where can we apply that information in our own operations?

  - How can we best do that?

- Where in our operations do you feel we can develop a stronger Wellness Culture? Where do elephants currently reside in our organization (or meetings, projects . . .)?

- How can we apply the information from the selection we read to eliminate the elephant in this area?

- How will eliminating the elephant in this area allow us to execute our strategies more effectively?

  - What additional and important outcomes will we generate by taking leadership action in this area?

- Are there places where we can or should replicate the successes we identified earlier?

- What do we want to achieve before our next elephant-stomping group meeting?

  - Why is achieving the above important?

- Optional: Where have we been applying these tools with our families?

  - What sorts of results are we creating?

  - How can we create an even stronger culture at home?

Do you have other strategies that can help us implement these tools to create an elephant-free office?

When you visit our Web site, www.stomptheelephant.com you will find additional methods, such as a mentor process and a self-directed study guide, which have helped thousands integrate, sustain and leverage these tools and their Wellness Culture.

Can I use the elephant-stomping group format at home, in my church, or in my community?

Many people currently do this and benefit from it. These are people who understand that the most important leadership work does not happen between the hours of 9:00 A.M. and 5:00 P.M.

For Further Information

*Verus Global Inc. wants to help
other companies create vibrant, high-performance
Wellness Cultures. For information, please call
1-800-569-1877 (U.S.A. only);
1-303-577-0075;
or e-mail info@verusglobal.com.*

APPENDIX B

The Elephant-Free Office Tool Box

Cut out the next page and carry it with you or post it as a reminder. This quick reference guide will assist you in selecting the appropriate Wellness Culture tool to help break your Leadership Lock—and remove the elephant in the office.

The 3 Conditions that Support Change

#1
Participants in the change process
feel good about themselves.

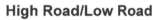

#2	EFFECTIVE CHANGE	**#3**
The process includes participants' ideas.		The process includes participants' motivations.

www.pathwaystoleadership.com

✂ -

High Road/Low Road
Awareness Muscle - Magic Moment

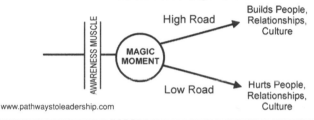

High Road → Builds People, Relationships, Culture

MAGIC MOMENT

Low Road → Hurts People, Relationships, Culture

AWARENESS MUSCLE

www.pathwaystoleadership.com

✂ -

The 3 Mind Factors

1. We can only focus on one thing at a time.
2. The mind cannot avoid a "don't."
3. We go toward what we focus on.

www.pathwaystoleadership.com

✂ -

ENERGY MAP

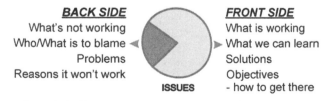

BACK SIDE	***FRONT SIDE***
What's not working	What is working
Who/What is to blame	What we can learn
Problems	Solutions
Reasons it won't work	Objectives
ISSUES	- how to get there

www.pathwaystoleadership.com

Questions Trigger the Mind

By asking questions
you can direct a person's focus
- including your own.

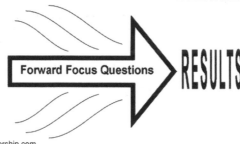

Forward Focus Questions RESULTS

The Humanity Factor

When people care enough
about other human beings
it influences all their interactions.